From Cluttered to Clear
in Just One Year

From Cluttered to Clear in Just One Year

Your Room-by-Room Home Makeover

By Debbie Bowie

Certified Organizer Coach (C.O.C.),
Certified Professional Organizer (C.P.O.),
and Certified Feng Shui Practitioner

DEBBIE BOWIE
Organizing and Coaching

Copyright © 2017 by Debbie Bowie

All Rights Reserved.

No part of this book may be reproduced or transmitted in any form or by any means, graphic, electronic, or mechanical, including photocopying, recording, taping, or by any information storage retrieval system, without the written permission of the author.

ISBN: 978-0-692-95703-5

For information contact:
Debbie Bowie
Debbie Bowie Organizing & Coaching
Tel: 804-730-4991
www.DebbieBowie.com

Table of Contents

Acknowledgements 11
Introduction 17
   Book Layout 19
   How to Use This Book 21

CHAPTER 1: Clutter Clearing 23
   Why Clear Clutter? 23
   Clutter Clearing Is a Complex Process 26
   Where Not to Start 27
   The Best Way to Start 29
   How to Clear Clutter 30
   Things to Be Purged 31
   Get Started 34

CHAPTER 2: Bedrooms 37
   Adult Bedrooms Feng Shui: How Quiet Is Your Bedroom? 38
   Clutter Clearing in the Bedroom Begins with Your Bed 41
   Top of the Dresser Clutter 43
   Create Good Feng Shui in the Bedroom with Art 45
   Banishing Shoes from the Bedroom Is Possible 46

From Cluttered to Clear in Just One Year

Live Within Your Closets, Drawers, and Cabinets If You
    Want to Live Peacefully 48
Where Is Your Dirty Clothes Hamper? 49
Clear Kid Photo Clutter: Who Are You Sleeping With? 50
Adult Bedroom Clutter Clearing Plan.................................... 52
Children's Bedroom Clearing Children's Toys 56
Feng Shui Challenges in Children's Rooms 58
Create Good Feng Shui in Children's Rooms........................... 60
Teach Children to Live Clutter-Free 63
Sleep: The Primary Function of Children's Bedrooms 66
Moms, Let Kids Get Rid of Belongings.................................... 68
Children's Rooms Clutter Clearing Plan 69

CHAPTER 3: Kitchen 75
Kitchen Clutter Clearing: How to Start................................... 76
Kitchen Clutter Clearing: Where to Start 78
Whose Kitchen Is It Anyway?.. 79
Want Peace in the Family? Clear Kitchen Countertops! 81
Kitchen Clutter: Reducing Duplicates 82
Cookbook Clutter: Let Go of the Fantasy................................ 84
The "Junk" Drawer: The Mini-Attic in the Kitchen 86
Counter Knife Blocks: A Feng Shui Kitchen No-No! 87
Ten Steps to Clutter Clearing Your Kitchen Desk 88
Kitchen Clutter Clearing Plan.. 92

CHAPTER 4: Bathrooms 95
Bathroom Feng Shui: An Energy and Organizing
    Challenge.. 96
Make Your Bathroom Counter Clutter Vanish! 98

Table of Contents

Bathroom Drawers: Mini-Organizing Nightmares.................. 100
Is Your Bathroom Vanity Cabinet a Toiletry Dump?.............. 103
The Bathroom Closet: Challenges and Solutions 105
Bathroom Clutter Clearing Plan.. 109

CHAPTER 5: Home Office 113
How Does Your Home Office Make You Feel?........................ 114
Your Home Office Is the Brain of Your Home 116
Three Important Steps to Unpacking Boxes in Your
   Home Office 118
Tips for Finding Calm Out of Home Office Chaos 119
Uncovering Your Emotional Blocks 121
Jumpstart Your Life; Clear Your Dead Computers 123
Seven Home Office Self-Seduction Tips 124
Do the Images in Your Workspace Support Success?............. 127
Tackling Dead Bodies (Difficult Tasks) in Your
   Home Office 129
Establish Home Office Boundaries and Expectations............. 132
Home Office Clutter Clearing Plan.. 133

CHAPTER 6: Living Room/Family Room 141
Family Room Family Room: The <u>Second</u> Heart of Your Home.. 142
Determine the Function of Your Family Room 143
How to Ensure Peace in Your Family Room 144
Family Room Dilemma: Noise Clutter 146
How Do You Solve the CD/DVD Dilemma?........................... 147
Is It Okay to Have Paper in Your Family Room? 149
How to Enhance Your Family Room 150
How to Bring Life Back to Your Living Room 153

Family/Living Room Clutter Clearing Plan.. 156

CHAPTER 7: Utility Room.. 163
"Utility Room" Does Not Have to Equal "Ugly Room"............. 163
Utility Room Functions: From Laundry to Cat Boxes.............. 165
Utility Rooms: Creating Calm in a Practical Place 167
Keep Utility Areas Looking and Smelling Clean...................... 168
Utility Room Clutter Clearing: Have Your Cleaning
    Products Had Babies?.. 169
Create a Utility Room You Love.. 170
Utility Room Clutter Clearing Plan.. 174

CHAPTER 8: Dining Room... 179
What Is the Function of Your Dining Room? 179
Why Dining Rooms Become Dumping Rooms 181
Dining Room Associations: Who Is Hanging Out at
    Your Family Gatherings? 182
China Cabinet/Dining Room Corner Cupboard:
    A Haven for Treasures or for Trash? 183
How to Avoid the "Eat and Run" Dining Room 185
Reclaim Your Dining Room Table 186
Ways to Give a Stagnant Dining Room New Life.................... 188
Art in the Dining Room 190
Create a Dining Room for Comfort and Connectedness 191
Dining Room Clutter Clearing Plan 194

Table of Contents

CHAPTER 9: Guest Room 197
- The Holidays Are Coming: Is Your Guest Room Ready?.......... 197
- Guest Room Functions: A Challenge of Competing Energies.. 198
- The Guest Room: Static or Cluttered 200
- Setting Up a "No Dumping" Multi-Purpose Guest Room........ 201
- *Guest Room Clutter Clearing Plan* 203

CHAPTER 10: Basement 207
- Ways to Approach Basement Clutter Clearing.....................207
- How to Avoid a Basement Dump 210
- Creating a Home Office in the Basement 211
- Enhancing a Basement... 212
- *Basement Clutter Clearing Plan* 215

CHAPTER 11: Garage... 219
- How to Create a Clutter-Free Garage 219
- The Condition of Your Garage Affects Your Life 220
- Garage Clutter Clearing: The Challenge of Negative Energies.. 221
- Garage Clutter Clearing: Trash First 223
- Need a Garage Update?...225
- The Overwhelming Garage: Seven Steps to Get Started 226
- Garage Organization: The Power of Categories 229
- A Great Greeting Is Good Feng Shui in a Garage 232
- The Ultimate in Good Garage Feng Shui.................................234
- *Garage Clutter Clearing Plan*...236

CHAPTER 12: The Attic 245
- The Ultimate Challenge: The Attic! 245
- Attic Clutter Clearing: Get Help 247
- What Does Not Belong in Your Attic? 249
- Love Your Attic 250
- Why Keep an Attic Clean? 251
- The Right Stuff for Good Feng Shui in Your Attic 252
- A New Vision for Your Attic 254
- *Attic Clutter Clearing Plan* 256

CHAPTER 13: Closets 267
- The Closet Decluttering Debate: Pull Everything
  Out or Not? 267
- Your Personal Closet Is a Reflection of You! 269
- Do You Have a Closet from Hell? 270
- Specialized Closet Design: Is It Worth the Cost? 274
- How to Create a Closet with Good Energy 276
- Six Common Issues That Hinder Maintaining
  Organized Closets 277
- *Closet Clutter-Clearing Plan* 282

CHAPTER 14: Getting Help 287
- Body Double 289
- Professional Organizer 290
- Coach 293

CHAPTER 15: Last Words 297

Acknowledgements

This book is proof that you never know where you'll end up when you take a step forward. That step for me was my decision to create a membership site named "The Clutter Clearing Community" in 2012. I wanted to have online conversations with people about the challenges and solutions of clearing clutter. That decision led to the creation of the content of this book.

The idea for the membership site was mine, but figuring out how to create, promote, market and maintain the site was completely out of my knowledge and skill set. Fortunately, the Universe provides when the time is right, and I was blessed to be working with Theresa Stenger of Stenger Design to market my business. I shared my idea of doing a membership site and asked if she would be willing to partner with me to make it happen. She took a big leap of faith and agreed to work with me

From Cluttered to Clear in Just One Year

to create and run the site. For over a year I wrote the content and Theresa made sure it got out on the site and in front of prospects. Together we worked to share the message, Clear Clutter for Good®.

This book would not have emerged in digital and physical form had it not been for Theresa's idea for the content. It was her suggestion that each month I choose a specific room of the house as the month's focus and write six to eight blog posts about common clutter and feng shui challenges in that space. By the end of a year I had written about every interior space in most houses. Theresa also suggested that I write step-by-step plans for clearing clutter in each area of the home. Those plans became the final pages of each chapter.

I cannot thank Theresa enough for her ideas that led to the creation of the content of this book. I'm also so grateful for her hard work creating, marketing, and promoting the site. Most important was her on-going support, being the "wind beneath my wings" that kept me writing from 2012 to 2013.

After writing the content of a book the next challenge is to have it edited. I had to be creative to get the editing done. Financial constraints made it impossible to hire an editor to proof my work, give feedback and recommend changes.

Again, the Universe let me know that bringing this project to completion was important by delivering three volunteer editors: Judy Proffitt, Cara Kinning, and Kate Culver. Each spent hours of their time reading through the text, catching typos and offering invaluable suggestions to get the book ready for publication. Their generosity with time and expertise was invaluable to me.

Judy Proffitt, a participant in one of my programs, took the first look at my rough draft. Her job was probably the most difficult because the first draft was pretty rough. With determination, commitment and te-

Acknowledgements

nacity she whipped it into shape. I so appreciated her candid suggestions to create a well-written manuscript.

Cara Kinning, a former professional organizer, accomplished editor, and good friend took the next swing at the project. She made many important suggestions to improve the text. She also formatted the text, a task that required incredible attention to detail. It was a task way beyond my abilities. Cara's biggest contribution, however, was naming the book. Coming up with creative, descriptive names is not my strong suit, so I was thrilled when Cara suggested the current title. It perfectly describes the content of the book.

Kate Culver, http://songtogaia.com/, a self-employed friend and accountability buddy in a mastermind group we both participated in, followed my progress with the book which I often discussed in our group. When I shared with her that I wanted one more reading after I finished my final edits, she volunteered to do the final edit. Thankfully she found a few more typos that I completely missed. Plus, she got the editing done in record time.

I owe a huge debt of gratitude to Laura Posey, formerly of Dancing Elephants and now owner of Simple Success Plans, http://simplesuccessplans.com/, who referred me to Joan Greenblatt a freelance designer with Upwork. Without Joan's assistance designing my book cover, formatting the book both for Kindle Direct Publishing and CreateSpace publication, plus uploading the manuscript to both platforms, progress on the book could have stalled indefinitely. Joan took me across the finish line with a cover I love and a steady stream of instruction and support to handle all the final decisions and details. She also shared a wealth of knowledge about how to market the book. I recommend her to anyone who has a manuscript ready for publication, without reservation.

Laura also made time to coach me on the best ways to market the

From Cluttered to Clear in Just One Year

book, a task that makes my head spin and can be totally overwhelming for me. I so appreciate her support of my work through the years, her wise counsel, and her specific recommendations for how to make this book available to a ready audience.

My husband, Bob, has been my ever-available cheerleader and strong source of support for all my creative endeavors. He was also my consultant when I'd get stuck and needed a good idea to keep moving. His belief in me and what I do makes it possible to keep writing and creating books like this.

Taking on a project as big as writing this book would not have been possible without the invaluable support of friends who believe in me and what I do. In addition to those I've mentioned above, I want to thank Shirley T. Burke, Theresa Stenger, Dale Burrell, Pam Williams, Cindy Beacham, Diane Thomson, Cheryl Susman, Veronique Eberhart, Chantell Vermaak-Johnson, and Dyanne Joyner.

A special thanks goes to my dad, Russ Randall. Dad has always taken risks to do what he felt was important to do. Over and over I watched him go from vision to action to completion, despite any obstacles or nay sayers. From him I learned to go for what I want even if I don't know how I'm going to get there. That certainly was my experience with this book. I learned that it's OK to paint outside the lines if that's what it takes to be my authentic self in alignment with my values and dreams. Feng shui definitely isn't a mainstream topic! When I finished my first book I gave him a copy. He opened it immediately and began reading—at the dinner table! He also bought 100 copies and gave them to everyone he knew, even the servers at McDonalds. His support and appreciation of what I'd done meant more to me than I can even express. Memories of his enthusiasm about my first book helped me persevere to complete this book. And, finally, I'm grateful to have inherited his creative brain

Acknowledgements

and sensibilities and for his encouragement that I use those gifts in my life.

Finally, my head cheerleader and source of love and support for 62 years of my life was my mom, Lyn Reid Randall Arrix. As a young girl, she told me I could do anything I set my mind to. As a young girl she urged me to have something for myself, so I wouldn't be dependent on a man. Without her ever-present love, appreciation of who I am and what I do, and belief that I was capable of great things, attempting a project of this magnitude would not even have landed on my radar. She set the stage for building a solid internal foundation that generated the courage, determination, and perseverance necessary to start and finish this book. Thanks, Mom!

Introduction

Do you love your home? The way it looks? The way it feels? Most of us are not conscious about whether we love our home or not. Our lives are moving so fast that we barely have time to bring our home into full focus. Home for many has become a place where you dump your stuff, recover from over-packed schedules, and sleep. That frantic lifestyle has led to serious clutter challenges for many people, unless they have an organized stay-at-home spouse, parent, or housekeeper. Work and outside activities eat up the time that could be spent maintaining a clean, organized, and comfortable home. The belief that "I'll get to it later. This is more important," has led many people to create homes that they tolerate but that they don't love; homes that don't feel good to them.

Feng shui, the Chinese art of placement, teaches that the condition of your home has a direct effect on the quality of your life. What you have in your space and how those things are arranged can support you and attract good into your life. Or, they can be draining, negatively affecting your energy, motivation, health, career, and relationships.

Your home is an outward extension of you. It reflects who you are, your values, and what has happened and is currently happening in your life. Feng shui teaches that if a home is tended lovingly every day as an essential part of your life, if it is organized and maintained with minimal clutter, and if it contains more positive sources of energy (e.g., items you love or use) and fewer sources of negative energy (e.g., clutter, broken things), it will attract good experiences and circumstances into your life, because **like energies attract.**

The converse is also true. A cluttered, disorganized, and/or neglected home will attract more challenges into your life. Negative energies attract negative experiences and circumstances. Therefore, if you want to create the conditions to attract positive circumstances and good opportunities into your life, it is essential that you clear clutter, enhance your space, and maintain a well-organized, comfortable home.

This book is the result of a year of writing blog posts for a membership site I once sponsored. The theme of the site was Clear Clutter for Good®, your good, the good of your family, and the good of your community. I combined feng shui wisdom with organizing principles in posts written to address all the major areas of a home.

Initially the articles were written with the idea that they be a guide to anyone who wanted to clear clutter from their home in 12 months. However, it soon became apparent to me that most people are unwilling or unable to invest so much time to caring for their home. That led me to combine the articles to create a reference manual for clearing clutter and creating a home with good feng shui. This book is intended as a guide

Introduction

for use when readers are motivated to improve the condition of any part of their home. The information in this book comes from my knowledge of feng shui and organizing principles, and years of experience doing hands-on organizing and feng shui consultations in clients' homes. It is intended to help you look at your space with fresh eyes and an awareness that everything you have in your space is alive with energies that affect the quality of your life.

What You Need to Know About This Book

Book Layout

Chapter 1 of this book is an overview of how to clear clutter. It is intended to give you a foundation of knowledge about the clutter clearing process to assist you in understanding the nature of the beast: what works, what doesn't, and how to make progress despite the complexity of clutter clearing.

I am often asked for my recommendation about where to start clearing clutter. I recommend starting in areas you use the most, so you can immediately benefit from your clutter clearing efforts. I also factor in the importance of the functions of particular rooms. For example, the energy in your bedroom has a direct effect on your quality of sleep, and therefore your health. Because having good health affects all other areas of your life, I recommend starting there.

The order of the chapters of this book was determined by the same criteria. Because good health affects all other aspects of your life, I start with the bedrooms, adult and children's bedrooms. Clearing the bedroom creates the conditions for good sleep and, consequently, for good health.

Next, I chose the kitchen because it is the heart of the home, the gathering place, the place of nurturance and sustenance. Clearing the kitchen is associated with getting fuel for your body and connection with other family members.

The home office is the place where you can organize your affairs (financial, insurance, medical records, etc.). Clearing and organizing that space gives you peace of mind.

We then go to the family room/living room, because those rooms are gathering places where people spend a lot of time. The utility room is also used frequently, to do laundry, to access cleaning and pet supplies, and to retrieve tools and hardware, etc.

The dining room and guest room are rooms that are often used only occasionally; therefore, they come at the end of the list of rooms inside your house.

I deliberately address basements, garages, and attics at the end of the book because they are three spaces where you definitely do not want to start clutter clearing. Most people don't spend much time in those spaces, and they are usually large spaces prone to being used as dumping spots for things you don't want to deal with, things you need to get rid of but can't part with, and storage of items you may or may not need. They are huge projects that are best addressed when you have the success of clearing the rest of your house behind you. Your success in other parts of your home can motivate you to figure out how to break down those big projects into manageable steps.

Introduction

How to Use This Book

There is no right or wrong way to use this book. It was initially written as a guide to clear and enhance your home over a 12-month period.

You can read the chapters in order and commit to working in a different area each month. However, it may not be possible to completely clear a room in a month. Alternatively, you can use the chapter topics and clutter clearing plans as guides to get some clearing done in each area over a 12-month period.

You can also use this book as a reference whenever you want to do some clutter clearing. Just open to the chapter about the space you plan to tackle to get ideas about how to handle your current clearing project.

You will notice repetition of certain phrases and recommendations throughout the book. This was done intentionally because it's quite possible that some readers will open the book to the chapter they need, missing out on key principles of clutter clearing and feng shui that are covered in earlier chapters. Repetition is very apparent in the clutter clearing plans because the clutter clearing process I recommend can be applied to all areas of the home.

Each chapter is meant to give you information and ideas about how to clear and enhance a particular area of your home. As you move through the book, you will move through the major areas of your whole house.

If you are a person who can't work in a straight line or finish a project, do not worry! Any clearing you do shifts energies in your space from negative to positive, as long as you remove cleared items from your space. You are not aiming for perfection in your clearing efforts. You are aiming for progress and movement. Progress, not perfection. Movement

From Cluttered to Clear in Just One Year

of items you no longer love or use out of your home makes space for new good things to come to you.

CHAPTER 1

Clutter Clearing

"When we clear the physical clutter from our lives, we literally make way for inspiration and 'good, orderly direction' to enter."
—Julia Cameron

Why Clear Clutter?

A Clutter-Free Home is a Healthy Home

Our homes are comparable to our bodies. We survive by taking in food, air, and water, and by excreting waste on a daily basis. Being healthy requires that we take in good food, air, and water. If we take in things that are not good for us such as unhealthy foods, polluted air, and toxic substances like excessive alcohol and drugs, over time we become sick. If our organs that eliminate waste and toxic substances (the liver and kidneys, in particular) become diseased and stop working properly, toxins back up in our system and we become sick.

Our houses, like our bodies, are living entities. Things quite naturally flow into our houses. You don't even have to work at getting things to come in. To become more conscious of this influx of things into your home, I invite you to consciously notice the quantities of things coming into your home in one day. At the very least there will be mail. Add to that the flow of personal items for every family member. And, if you are into shopping, watch out! Day after day of that influx results in an increasing accumulation of things. Without being conscious of it, and without conscious effort to manage the flow of those items, your house begins filling up.

Healthy homes, like healthy bodies, are those in which there is a regular flow of things both in and out. Ideally there is a regular release of waste in the form of garbage and recycling. However, that's definitely not enough to keep a house healthy. That is just the tip of the iceberg. To keep the energy of a house looking and feeling good, there must also be a regular outflow of things that are no longer used or loved.

You might be saying, "Duh! I know that! Of course, stuff must go out." But, are you deliberately doing it? Many of us have gotten so busy with the pressing demands of work, raising a family, dealing with ailing parents, and keeping up with regular maintenance tasks, that we are not conscious of the press of our belongings. We keep stuffing things in closets, drawers, attics, garages, and basements to ease the pressure, but we never really relieve it! We think we don't have time to address the quantities of stuff that are building up.

Guess what? The enormity of the task increases exponentially the longer you put off doing it. And, you pay a hefty price! The more things you have in your house that no longer serve you, the sicker your house becomes. Sick houses affect the people who live in them! For example, clients of mine who have the most stuff have a higher incidence of chronic illness (fibromyalgia, depression, anxiety) than do clients with fewer possessions.

Clutter Clearing

Like the human body, to maintain a healthy house you *must* excrete waste on a regular basis. Waste in the home or office includes garbage and recycling plus anything that no longer serves you; anything that you no longer love or use. Many things you save because "I might need this someday" fall into this category: the odd part, the bit of string, the ancient appliance that you never use, etc. You save them but fail to organize them for easy access, so they take on dead, negative energies.

Clearing Clutter Creates Mental Clarity

I remember walking into a client's packed home office. It looked like a used furniture warehouse with the addition of large quantities of paper and cosmetics strewn about. As I scanned the room, I noticed that my brain froze. I could not figure out where to begin clearing. That's what happens in spaces with too much stuff in them which results in large quantities of negative energy. The thinking part of the brain just shuts off.

This was particularly troubling to me, because I was a paid professional hired for my expertise in clearing clutter and organizing spaces. What I did that day, and continue to do when my brain gets stuck, is 1) get still and 2) pray for guidance. The guidance I got was: "What would I recommend that a client do in a similar situation?" The answer to that question was: "Remove something big from the room." Removing something sizable stirs up the stuck energies and make it possible to think again. I removed one large piece of furniture and the balance of energies in the room shifted from negative to positive, just enough to reignite my thinking. With that item gone, I was able to access my knowledge and wisdom, and we were off and running.

Clearing clutter creates mental clarity. Feng shui teaches that everything is alive with energy and that energy talks to you either positively or negatively. Every single item in your space chatters at you all the time. The more stuff you have in a room, the more conversations will be distracting you. When you reduce the number of items in your space, you reduce conversations that distract and overwhelm you.

Clearing Clutter Makes Space for New, Good Things to Come to You

If your space is packed to the gills, there is no space for new, good things to come to you. You cannot attract more positive things and opportunities into your life. When you clear out items you no longer love or use, you free up space to attract more of what you really want in life.

A client of mine wanted to sell more memberships for the golf club that employed her. With that goal in mind she cleared clutter from her apartment. Within weeks she made more sales than she had in months. Clearing out things that no longer served her freed space and energy to achieve her sales goal.

Clutter Clearing Is a Complex Process

Clearing clutter is no big deal if your home is well-organized and you have been diligent about daily cleanup and maintenance of your home over time. But, if your home has never been well-organized and/or if the organization has melted down over time, plus you have given in to thoughts of "I'm too tired; I'll do it later"; "I'll never get this done," then the thought of clutter clearing, even for your own benefit, can be overwhelming. Where will you start? How will you start? How can you keep yourself engaged in a process that at best takes a lot of time and at worst is utterly daunting?

Clutter Clearing

Clutter clearing is a complex process even for the most motivated individual. It involves physical, special, logistical, and emotional challenges. It comes easily to some people and can seem impossible to others. But, if clutter clearing has been postponed for some time, and there are quantities of clutter throughout your house, even those who find clutter clearing easy are likely to have difficulty facing their monster.

Why? Clutter holds negative energies (energies that make you feel bad), and *negative energies repel*. When there are small quantities of negative energy, it is easier to muster the motivation and drive to address them. However, when there are larger pockets of negative energy in multiple locations throughout your house, the total quantity of negative energy can be overwhelming and shut down cognitive function. The pre-frontal cortex of the brain (the area that houses executive functions like initiating action, prioritizing, decision making, and organizing) freezes. This results in an inability to figure out where to start, how to start, and even how to ask for help to get the task done.

Where Not to Start

Don't Start with Paper!

Why not start with paper? If you start with paper, you will quit. You'll run away! You'll go shopping, watch TV, eat a cake, or decide the lawn has to be mowed, right now. Paper will shut you down despite your best intentions. It's more difficult to clear than almost anything else. It takes a long time to see and feel results for your efforts, and it is one of the most boring things to clear. Do you think you could maintain your momentum and motivation through your project if you start with paper? No! It's more likely that you will become overwhelmed and quit.

The only way to effectively deal with paper is to back into it. In other words, don't tackle it head on. Have a blast evaluating, sorting, and purging everything else in your space first. Then, when the room is feeling great and all that's left to do is sort and clear paper, you'll find the paper easier to face and clear.

If there is paper mixed into the rest of your clutter, distracting you from getting any clutter clearing done, gather it together in a pile, bag or box. Set it aside to tackle when the rest of your space is clear and organized.

Don't Start with Attics, Basements, or Garages

Why not start with clearing out your attic, basement, or garage? You don't live in those areas. You will be more successful at initiating and sustaining clutter clearing efforts if you start in areas where you spend the most time. That way you will be able to feel the benefits of your efforts every day. The pleasure you experience in a less-cluttered space can motivate you to keep going and to maintain order.

Attics, basements, and garages are also large spaces that often contain large quantities of things to be sorted, evaluated, and organized. The quantity of items and size of the space can be overwhelming. It will also take much longer to see and feel progress in a large cluttered space.

In addition, those large spaces often the dirtiest place in your home and full of things seldom used that have dead, static, negative energies. The negative energies in the attic, garage, and basement will repel you, making it particularly difficult to motivate yourself to begin working in them.

Clutter Clearing

The Best Way to Start

Start with Big Stuff First

When tackling any organizing project like clutter clearing, it is imperative that you see visible progress immediately and do so without overwhelming yourself. Seeing progress is the only way to stay motivated to continue doing work that is challenging and overwhelming. Over time in my work with clients I learned that the best way to quickly see and feel progress and quell feelings of overwhelm was to start with big stuff. Big stuff includes furniture, audio-visual equipment, books, clothing, framed art, empty boxes, anything of significant size.

I've noticed that the clients I work with instinctively reach first for things that are the most difficult to address, probably because those things "talk" the loudest and have the most distracting and demanding negative energies. For example, they reach for paper, which just screams with negative energy. It does seem to make sense; normally getting the worst task done first is a good idea. But, because clearing clutter and getting organized is so challenging mentally, emotionally, and physically, the top priority must be to see visible results, which means dealing with things that are easy to sort and pitch. Easy is good. Easy leads to progress and movement, not overwhelm, mental paralysis and stagnation.

Do What Is Easiest!

I am sometimes asked if I ever get overwhelmed. My answer is always a resounding "Yes, of course!" However, I've learned to avoid overwhelm by looking for things that are big and easy to clear. By easy I mean things or categories of things that you have no emotional attachment to that you can get rid of without deliberation.

Because those things can be removed quickly, you'll be able to see and feel results quickly. That will motivate you to continue clearing.

How to Clear Clutter

Use the "Love It, Use It, or Lose It Method"

Terah Kathryn Collins introduced me to the idea that we thrive when we live with what we love or use. In her book, *The Western Guide to Feng Shui*, she recommends that you "love it or use it" if you plan to keep a particular item. I modified that statement to "Love It, Use It, or Lose It." In other words, when evaluating an item during clutter clearing, ask yourself, "Do I love this?" If you don't love the item, ask yourself, "Do I use it?" If again the answer is no, then consider losing it. Throw it away. Give it away. Clear it out of your space.

Love It

People tend to love things because they:

- Were a gift from a special person
- Hold a special memory
- Hold a special association
- Are aesthetically pleasing
- Engender a special feeling

People tend not to love items because they:

- Remind them of an unpleasant time or experience
- Remind them of someone they dislike or who dislikes them
- Have been outgrown, such as memorabilia, records, clothes, and sports equipment that are no longer of interest
- Are broken and not worth fixing or are too difficult to fix

Clutter Clearing

Use It

Using things gives them energy. The energy of an item that is not used goes dead over time, unless it has "love it" energy. Homes and offices are filled with things that have dead energies. One of the best ways to energize a space and thus energize the person working in the space is to clear out items that aren't being loved or used, leaving the space filled with only those things that are alive with energy. How often should you use something to keep its energy alive? A good standard is once a year.

Lose It

Items to lose are those that you don't love or use. Items that aren't used at least once a year often have a dead energy. It's easiest to feel the effects of dead energy once you have cleared things that you no longer love or use from a space. In the absence of dead things, you'll find yourself energized and ready to take action. Although you may not be conscious of which things have energies that have gone dead from disuse, those dead energies do affect your ability to be productive and think clearly.

Things to Be Purged

Broken Things

Broken things clearly are sources of negative energy. People usually have some uncomfortable feelings when looking at or dealing with something broken. You may feel irritated, annoyed, frustrated, burdened with one more task to be done, angry, or even tired.

Broken things hold the energy of brokenness and can energetically attract being broke (financially) or being physically broken (health problems). Remember, energy attracts more of the same. Broken things also require work on your part. First you have to decide if a broken item is worth fixing. If so, you have to figure out how to fix it. You might need to find someone to fix it. You might need to take it to a repair shop, and on and on. Do you get the picture? The best way to handle broken things is to either fix them quickly, if they are worth fixing, or dispose of them.

Static Things

The word "static" is defined as "lacking in movement, action, or change, especially in a way viewed as undesirable or uninteresting." Static things don't move, and things that don't move are more likely to have dead energies. The exception, of course, is something that you love. Many things that are loved don't move, but are alive with energy because of their aesthetic qualities or positive associations. However, if a static item is not something you love, and it's not being used at least once a year, it's likely to have a dead energy and is a candidate for trash or donation.

You can find static things in every room of your house, in every closet, cabinet and drawer. The common categories of static things often found in large quantities in a home are: paper, books, memorabilia (the kind you find in boxes in the attic), clothing, and photos. Of these categories, be sure to start your clearing with one that is easy for you to do. As we already discussed, don't start with paper unless it is the only thing you need to clear.

Anything with a Negative Association

When you look at an item and it reminds you of a person or an event that makes you feel mad or sad, it has a negative association.

As you move through your space, check out the associations of everything. Pay particular attention to the first thoughts that pop into your head when looking at an object. Those thoughts often hold the primary association. Are those thoughts positive or negative?

By getting rid of anything with a negative association, you clear negative energies and create a space in which to thrive and attract more good things to you.

Make Things Go Away Quickly

Make "lose it" items leave as quickly and easily as possible. The most important thing to remember about the "lose it" step in the "Love It, Use It, or Lose It" method is that the full benefits of clearing occur only after you've removed the items that you want to "lose" from your space, including your car. If those items are still anywhere in your space, you won't receive the full benefit of the clearing.

Trust that items you plan to give away will end up in exactly the right new home without you having to make it so. It's not important that those items be given to exactly the right person. In fact, insisting on giving away your things to many different people or locations can be a way to resist letting go of your things. Why? Because the more deliveries you have to make, the less likely you are to make them due to the energy and time required to do so. Plus, you are postponing the benefits of clutter clearing. Choose a charity, drop your things off, and let go.

Unless you are a "get it done" kind of person who can put together a yard sale in a matter of days, don't hold onto things for a yard sale. Saving things for a yard sale is like building a concrete wall around yourself, blocking the flow of new good things to you. It's rare that yard sales happen quickly because doing one requires that it be the right time of year, planning and advertising, and accumulating sufficient items to make your effort worthwhile. I sometimes find prospective yard sale items hanging around in garages years after they were identified as yard sale items. Release those items and watch your life start moving again!

From Cluttered to Clear in Just One Year

Get Started

You promised yourself that today is the day you would tackle the clutter in your home. You wake up thrilled at the prospect, right? Wrong! No one wants to spend their precious spare time sorting through the debris of their lives? So, how do you get yourself to do it? Promises aren't enough. Good intentions aren't enough.

Below is a simple process that can help you get started when you have lots of clutter and feel overwhelmed.

Five-Step Clutter Clearing Process
1. **Remember that doing something is better than doing nothing.** What you do may not produce stunning results quickly, but doing any clearing shifts energies in a positive direction.
2. **Set a small goal.** For example, plan to work for ten minutes. Set a timer and go to work. When the timer goes off, stop. Most of us can work for ten minutes. During that time do whatever is easiest to create some new order. Throwing away trash is usually easy. Clearing off a table might be easy. Finding a bag full of things to give away might be easy.
3. **Start with the biggest items in the space you are clearing and use the Love It, Use It or Lose It** clutter clearing method. Check the energy of big things. Ask yourself, "Do I love this?" If you have no special emotional attachment to the item, ask yourself, "Do I use this?" If the answer is "no" or "not in the last year," consider losing it.

As soon as you decide to eliminate an item, remove it

from the space, preferably by placing it just outside the door. It's not a good idea to pause in the evaluation process to take the item much further than outside the door, because you risk getting sidetracked doing something else.

Removing the item from the room releases the energy that the item was holding. That released energy is then available to use as you continue making decisions about what to keep and what to release. As you make decisions and move things out of the room, your energy increases and making decisions becomes easier. Your brain begins to generate creative new ideas about what you can do in your space.

When you find that removing things from the room is getting difficult because of the quantity of items outside the door, stop sorting. Reward yourself by taking those items to their respective locations. DO NOT stop to reorganize the new location if you cannot easily put things away. Leave items in the areas where they belong and make a mental note that the area needs your attention, at a later date. Then, return to your project.

4. **Congratulate yourself on your success.** That sounds silly, doesn't it? Some of you are thinking, "So, I did ten minutes of clearing in a house that needs ten weeks of clearing. What's the big deal?" The big deal is that you made a plan to clear and kept it. You got started. Every bit of work helps. Besides, whenever you complete a task your brain rewards you with a shot of serotonin, the "feel good" neurotransmitter. Plus, if you don't stop and feel the good feelings that come from the accomplishment of the work, it will be difficult to motivate

yourself to keep clearing. It's a head game. Play it!
5. **Schedule your next clearing session, preferably sooner rather than later.** Repeat the process. All progress makes a difference, as long as you aren't creating more chaos between clearing sessions than the amount you cleared.

It sounds so simple, doesn't it? If that's the case, why do people avoid decluttering? How do their spaces become nightmares right before their eyes? The fact that something sounds simple doesn't make it easy to do. Clutter clearing involves making so many decisions. You not only need to decide what to keep and what to pitch, but also where to start and what to do with all your things as you work. It can be a great logistical challenge with the potential for distraction everywhere.

When I work with clients, part of my job is to keep them from running away. Even though I am in charge of the process and of making it easier for them, they are still affected by the way the space feels and by the enormity of the decision-making process. Your job is to keep yourself clearing despite the urge to run away.

CHAPTER 2

Bedrooms

"I'd always want to decorate my bedroom. I needed visuals and to be stimulated by things. I'm still like that. It's the way I see the world."
—Rob Zombie

As mentioned earlier, I recommend the bedroom as a good starting point for clearing the rooms of your house. Why? Because you spend more time in that space than in any other part of your house. When you sleep, you are in one spot for six to eight hours. That means your body is exposed to the energy of your bedroom for six to eight hours, long enough to significantly affect you.

How is the typical bedroom treated by its occupants? From what I've observed in the homes of clients, it is susceptible to dumping by busy occupants, and often houses many things that don't fit the functions of the room (sleep, changing your clothes, and intimacy). Frequently it is one of the last spaces to be decorated and decluttered.

A clutter-free, peaceful, and nicely appointed bedroom will expose you to positive energies that will make for good sleep. A cluttered bedroom, which usually has its share of dust and grime, will be filled with negative energies that over time can negatively affect your immune system and your health. The state of your health affects every other part of your life. So, clearly, bedrooms really are a high priority for clutter clearing.

I have broken this section into two parts, adult bedrooms and children's bedrooms, because they each have specific challenges. However, much of what I write about in the adult bedrooms section can also be applied to children's bedrooms.

Adult Bedrooms

Feng Shui: How Quiet Is Your Bedroom?

A starting point for organizing any room is to identify the function of the space. What kinds of activities are going to happen there? Those activities then guide your decision-making about what to keep in the space.

Bedrooms usually have three primary functions:
- Rest
- Changing clothes
- Intimacy

In my work as a professional organizer, I've had the opportunity to see some bedrooms that include everything but the kitchen sink. How anyone could get a good night's sleep in one of those rooms is beyond me!

Bedrooms

Feng Shui teaches that everything is alive with energy. Everything!
Energies are positive or negative, and the energy of things talks to you. This may sound silly or "woo woo," like questionable "New Age" nonsense to you, but stick with me. Every item around you gets its energy from its attributes: color, material, texture, design, and even memories associated with it. Therefore, when an item is left out in the open, all of its components are visible, and its energy is talking or "chattering" away at you.

For example, a pair of pants dropped on the floor could say, "Why don't you hang me up?" or "The wife's not going to be happy that you've left me here!" Everything that is out and visible in a bedroom is talking to you... all at the same time! So, it only makes sense that there is an inverse relationship between the number of things that are visible in a bedroom and how peaceful the space feels.

Going a step further, there are specific types of items that are particularly noisy and problematic in a bedroom:
- **Work-related items** - Items associated with either your job or other responsibilities in your life call out to you, constantly, saying "You should be getting me done!" And, work-related items such as bills, sewing projects, exercise equipment, house plans, day planners, and computers in the bedroom can cause you to "work" in your dreams. The bedroom is about rest, not work. To make your bedroom a haven where quality rest is possible, remove everything that has to do with an activity or work.
- **Energy enhancers** - Mirrors, fountains, and televisions all have active energies and therefore should not be placed in

a bedroom where they may interfere with creating a restful environment. If you feel strongly about having a mirror in the bedroom, have only one. Fountains not only stir up the energies in a space, they have been known to cause the urge to urinate. Televisions stimulate both the nervous system and a person's thoughts. It is recommended that you stop watching television an hour or two before you turn out the lights to allow time for your nervous system to settle down. Besides, television affects intimacy. Instead of being focused on your spouse or partner you are focused on the screen.

- **Books** - There are five elements in feng shui, wood, water, fire, earth and metal. Each has a different energy level and can show up in different forms. Feng shui teaches that the words in books are fire elements. Fire elements are the most energetic of all elements. The paper of the pages is wood. Wood feeds fire. So, books are little bonfires! They have a stimulating, hot energy. Add to that the fact that when you are sleeping, your subconscious can access the content of the books. If your spouse likes to read war books, you're sleeping in a space that has the energy of war. Your brain is accessing the horror of the content of those books. Also, I believe that the negative energy of war books can lead to conflict between spouses. To manage the hot energy of books, I recommend that you keep just one to three books or magazines at your bedside. Limiting the quantity will limit the stimulation. I also recommend choosing books that are a gentle read, preferably positive stories with little emotional stress or violence.

- **Photographs** - Images of people in photographs are also fire elements. To make your bedroom peaceful, limit the photographs in the bedroom. Photographs add a great life-affirming energy in any other part of your house, but in the bedroom, they "talk" loudly and can disrupt sleep. Photos of your children can distract you from the opportunity for intimacy with your spouse. Photos of parents and children can keep your subconscious working on ideas for parenting and caregiving. Plus, the photos hold the energies of the people in them. Do you really want to be sleeping with your children or your parents?

How Quiet Is your Bedroom?

The condition of your bedroom can have a profound effect on your health. Because you daily spend more time in that one place than anywhere else, the noise of negative energies in the bedroom can affect the body negatively, resulting in health issues. Take steps to prevent sources of stimulation (work-related items, energy enhancers, books, photographs, etc.) from "talking" to you by moving them elsewhere. Make your bedroom a lovely, peaceful place to rest.

Clutter Clearing in the Bedroom Begins with Your Bed

Your Bed Should Be Utterly Comfortable.

Easily the biggest piece of furniture in the room, the bed can have a profound impact on both the health of its occupants and the quality of the relationship of a couple. It is important to consider the comfort of the mattress and the history of the mattress and bed frame.

I hope that you spend the recommended six to eight hours in bed sleeping, about one third of each day. If your bed is comfortable, you will rest well and awaken refreshed the next day. If it is not comfortable (too hard, too soft, dips in the middle, is hard to get in and out of), then the mattress is an irritant in direct contact with your body. Six to eight hours of discomfort can translate into exhaustion, irritability, depression, and disease. In order to thrive in life, you must sleep well. If your bed has passed its prime, and you find yourself having more and more aches and pains, consider pitching the old mattress and buying one that is as comfortable as you can afford.

What Is the History of your Headboard and Bed Frame?
Objects hold the energy of their history. If the history of your bed is positive to you and your partner, and you both love its style, great! Keep it.

If, however, one of you is concerned about its history or dislikes the style, it's a good idea to either move it to another room or get rid of it. A couple cannot afford to have a bed that one of them dislikes, for whatever reason. Those negative feelings will affect the relationship.

One client told me, "I think we should get rid of this bed. My husband slept in it with his ex-wife."

What do you think about that statement?

I'll never forget that day: I was standing in my client's master bedroom looking at that exquisite, ornately carved oak headboard. It was a beauty! My client was newly married and had invited me to help her clear clutter to make the master bedroom a place where she and her husband would be comfortable.

Bedrooms

"What's the history of the headboard and the mattress?" I asked. She informed me that the headboard was a family heirloom belonging to her husband, and that the mattress was, in fact, the one he'd slept on with his former wife. Clearly the energy of the bed screamed "ex-wife!" I recommended that she and her husband consider using the headboard and bed frame in a guest room, give away the mattress, and purchase a new bed or headboard and mattress, one that they both love.

"The mattress holds her energy," I said. "It's as if she's sleeping in the bed with the two of you." My client was thrilled with my recommendation and passed it on to her husband. He was skeptical at first. But, to his credit, he consulted the women in his office about the mattress situation. When he asked them if they thought it would be a problem for he and his new wife to be sleeping on the bed he'd slept in with his ex-wife, he got unanimous agreement that doing so would be a big mistake. Marriage can be challenging enough without having an ex-wife's energy hanging around, especially in the most intimate moments!

Clearing older furniture that holds negative energies from the bedroom can make all the difference in the effect the room has on you and your relationship.

Top of the Dresser Clutter

You may have learned this the hard way: it's best to leave clearing cluttered dresser tops for last in your bedroom clutter clearing efforts. Why? Those surfaces are usually covered with little stuff like jewelry, receipts, business cards, perfumes, coins, knick-knacks, photographs and anything else that lands on that tempting flat surface. If you begin clutter clearing with small stuff, you're more likely to get overwhelmed by the quantity of decisions to be made and the seeming impossibility of seeing visible progress quickly.

If, on the other hand, you figured out that it's best to tackle the rest of the room first, good for you! That way you have already improved the energy in your space to a point where facing that dreaded mess of little stuff on your dresser top seems possible.

So, you're looking at all that little stuff. Where do you begin? Guess what? You use the same process for that surface that you used for all the other areas of the room. Start by considering the function of that surface. In other words, what kinds of items do you want to have out in the open—either because you love them and they make your heart sing, or because you want easy access to them?

Once you make that decision, remove anything from the dresser top that doesn't fit that function. Move those items in the direction they need to go. For example, if business cards really belong in your home office, place the cards near the door to the room, ready for transport to the home office when you take a break or finish your work for the day. Don't take those items to the location at that moment. If you do, you may never get back to the dreaded dresser top!

Once you've removed the things that don't fit the dresser top function, sort the remaining items into categories of like items. Clump jewelry with jewelry, perfumes with perfumes, etc. That way you can get an accurate picture of the quantity of each category of items and are better able to decide how many of a particular type of item you want to have out in the open. Be very selective about those things that remain on the dresser top, because each is alive with an energy that will talk to you while you sleep. Remember, your bedroom will feel more restful if fewer items are visible.

Bedrooms

A great option for the dresser top is a box in which you can store all that little stuff that talks too loudly. Even men find a dresser box helpful for storing nail clippers and other small grooming tools, as well as various odds and ends that could get lost in the depths of drawers.

Dresser tops are best treated as decorative surfaces rather than as landing strips for the stuff in your pockets and anything you don't want to bother moving to its rightful home. Once you identify the function of the dresser top, it will be easier to stop yourself from just dropping anything in your hand or pocket onto that surface.

Clear your dresser top and then treat it with respect. The peace of your bedroom depends on it!

Create Good Feng Shui in the Bedroom with Art

What hangs on the walls of your bedroom? What kind of energy surrounds you when you sleep? The energy of each painting, print, and photograph affects the quality of your sleep and the quality of your relationships. In fact, the feng shui of any art in your bedroom is also directly related to your overall health and general well-being. Therefore, it's important to check out each piece of art to make sure that its energy is in keeping with the primary energy you want to achieve in the space.

Remember, bedrooms are primarily about rest, changing your clothes and intimacy (sex). So, ideally the art should have a restful, peaceful, and/or sensual energy. Landscapes, beach scenes, and garden scenes are good choices for a peaceful bedroom.

Important Feng Shui Factors to Consider When Choosing Bedroom Art

Check out the subject matter of each piece of art. What is going on in the scene? You are sleeping with the content. The best feng shui advice for bedroom art is to choose art that has peaceful content or that you want to see happening in your life. To ensure peace in the bedroom and restful sleep, remove anything that has a negative association or a busy, frenetic energy. Scenes with people should be avoided, because people are high energy fire elements. Violent or troubling scenes can affect your interactions with a spouse or partner and can disrupt your sleep. Definitely avoid depictions of war and anything disturbing. Also, avoid art that conveys sad or lonely images.

Choose art that evokes positive feelings and/or shows what you want to experience in the space. If, for example you want to attract romance, choose art that feels romantic. If you are part of a couple and want to add some spark to your love life, add prints of couples embracing, sensual subjects that you both find appealing, and pairs of objects such as lamps, prints or candles to create more "couple" energy. You can also make the bedroom all about the two of you by enlarging photographs from your wedding, honeymoon or a special trip you enjoyed together, framing them, and displaying them in the room. Avoid art depicting just one woman or one man, which can hold the energy of being single and could affect the strength of your relationship.

Banishing Shoes from the Bedroom <u>Is</u> Possible

As I've mentioned, your goal in setting up your bedroom is to create a space that is completely conducive to sleep. The energy of smelly feet can only be very distracting. Why then is it that I so often find pairs of shoes strewn across bedroom floors? **I'm fairly certain that part of the problem is not having adequate storage for the number of shoes that people own these days.**

Also, perhaps more often shoes just don't make it to the closet. You may be thinking, "Why put them away? I'm just going to put them on again tomorrow."

Sweaty, smelly feet and rest just don't go well together. Ideally, it's best to reduce the number of shoes you own to those that can easily fit in your closet; then make sure they are returned to their "home" every night. For one thing, you'll find your bedroom will be more peaceful because there will be fewer items out and visible. You'll also find that your focus will shift away from the "energy chatter" of stray shoes to more important things, such as some gentle reading, reflecting on your day, or intimate conversations and sex with a partner or spouse.

The energy chatter of shoes makes one of the following judgments:
- **Those shoes really are too tight**, but they are the only ones that really look professional.
- **I should polish that pair.** Look how scuffed they are!
- **The bottom of these shoes are really worn.** Is it time to bite the bullet and get another pair?
- **I look like such a dork in those shoes** . . . but they're so comfortable!
- **Those shoes really stink.** I wonder what's going on with my feet that they stink so badly.

With all those conversations going on, is it any wonder that you don't get great sleep anymore? Yes, when your eyes are closed you can't see all those shoes, but your subconscious can feel their energy even when you are sleeping. Their presence interferes with peaceful sleep.

So, banish shoes from the bedroom to the closet and enjoy the peace that results from your efforts. Remember, if you're coming up with *any* reason at all to "let go" of a pair of shoes—just do it. Set them free. Donate them to charity if they are in good condition or pitch them if are too worn out. You can also look for charities that refurbish shoes (www.shoeheals.org/) and give them to people in need.

Take the remaining shoes and find a storage solution that will work in your closet. Try a stacking shelf or, if wall space is limited, consider storing solutions that you can hang in the closet. Then, enjoy sweeter dreams!

Live Within Your Closets, Drawers, and Cabinets If You Want to Live Peacefully

I was raised with parents who were not accumulators of material things. I never saw clothes hanging from brackets attached to the outside of closets or scads of toiletries strewn across a bathroom counter. So, in my early days working as a professional organizer I was really unprepared for the quantities of clothes and other belongings that spilled from clients' closets, drawers, and cabinets.

As you know, feng shui teaches that everything has energy and the energy talks to you. When things that really belong in the privacy of a closet are hanging outside it, they talk to you!

In fact, when there are a number of them on the loose, they scream at you. The positive, peaceful energies of a clutter-free bedroom can shift into negative energies that feel like a noisy crowd in the presence of clothes that no longer fit in closets and drawers.

What to do? Live within your closets, drawers, and cabinets. Don't accumulate more than you can comfortably house in the storage options available to you. If you already have more things than can easily fit into your drawers, closets and cabinets, do a major purge (consider hiring a professional organizer to make this happen if it's too big a project for you), and release enough items so what you do keep can comfortably fit into available storage. "But my closets are so small," you say. Get a wardrobe! Clean out a closet in another room and move some of your clothes there! Redesign your closets. What do you really want: all those clothes, toiletries, gadgets, etc., or a peaceful bedroom where it is possible to rest?

Where Is Your Dirty Clothes Hamper?

At the end of the day, where do you throw your dirty clothes? I'm really hoping your answer is not, "On the floor of the bedroom!" Unfortunately, I know that is exactly where some clothes end up!

What I mean is, where do you keep your dirty clothes hamper or laundry basket? If one exists, I often find it out in the open in the bedroom. Think about the energy of dirty clothes. The fresh smell and feel of clean clothes is gone. Instead, dirty clothes hold body oils and odors, dirt, and sometimes grime. Do you really want to be sleeping with unconscious access to that type of energy? Even if you don't have offensive body odor, dirty clothes are just that … dirty! Their energy has changed from fresh and clean to rumpled and dirty.

If you have doubts about the negative effect of dirty clothes on the peaceful environment of a bedroom, temporarily move your dirty clothes hamper out of the room. Wait about five minutes for the energies stirred up by that change to settle. Return to the room and notice how it feels. The space likely will feel more peaceful and welcoming.

Look for a place to store your laundry basket that is near the bedroom, and make the effort every time you undress to walk over and put your dirty clothes in it. Possible locations are a bathroom, laundry room, or closet. In my home, I emptied out the bottom of our linen closet in the hall for our basket. The closet is just two steps outside our bedroom. If you just don't have space for it outside the bedroom, at least purchase and use a hamper with a lid.

Saying "no" to dirty clothes in the bedroom is saying "yes" to a fresher space that will promote relaxation and more restful sleep.

Clear Kid Photo Clutter: Who Are You Sleeping With?

"I recommend that you remove all photos of your children from your bedroom," I said to a woman who had hired me to do a feng shui consultation. She looked at me with a shocked expression, as though I'd just told her to strip naked. "Really? Why?" "Well," I responded, "those photos hold the energy of your children. It's as though you are sleeping with your children. Do you want to be sleeping with your children? Plus, how romantic can it be for you and your husband when your children seem to be looking on during your intimate moments?"

Like my client, you may be skeptical, but I challenge you to remove all photos from your bedroom except those of you and your spouse or partner. Make the bedroom's energy all about the two of you and see if the energy in your marriage shifts in a positive direction. If you set up

Bedrooms

the bedroom as a love nest, a place to honor and enjoy your relationship, you are likely to enhance the positive energy between the two of you.

Once you have children, an enormous amount of energy naturally shifts to meet the legitimate needs of the children. Tending the needs of the couple can easily slip by the wayside in the busyness of childrearing and making ends meet. Even the bedroom can become all about the children. In over a decade of helping people clear clutter and improve their lives and marriages, I've found that the couples with the most photos of their children in the bedroom often have no pictures of the two of them in that room! They aren't even conscious that they've left themselves out of the picture.

Given that the health of the couple assures the health of the family unit, doesn't it make sense that you devote one room to the two of you? Make sure that you have at least one photo of you and your partner or spouse in the bedroom. Remove all photos of people other than the two of you. Not only will your bedroom feel more peaceful once the crowd has exited the room, but you may also find it easier to focus on your relationship.

Most people want to know what to do with all the photos that they remove, as if the actual children were being asked to leave. I assure them that those photos can be displayed in any of the public areas of the home.

From Cluttered to Clear in Just One Year

Adult Bedroom Clutter Clearing Plan

You're standing in the doorway of your bedroom... Pay attention to both your thoughts and feelings as you take in your room. Do you like what you see? Is it a peaceful place? Or, do you find yourself thinking, "What a mess! Who could get a good night's sleep in this mess?" Are you feeling pleased, proud, and happy about the state of the space? Or is your gut clenching and your jaw tightening as you face the prospect of tackling the clutter in the space?

Clearing any room is rarely a linear process, but I am going to provide you with steps to take so you'll have a reference point to refer to if you get off track.

Use the following list as a flexible guide, not the "right way":
1. **Take a deep breath.** Actually, take several deep breaths and remind yourself of your intentions. You want to create a comfortable environment for sleep, changing your clothes, and intimacy/sex.
2. **Take several "before" pictures of the room.** You'll want to be able to brag about your progress to those in your life who can appreciate your hard work and commitment to clear clutter to create a comfortable, peaceful home. Before and after pictures are a great way to document progress and remind you to celebrate your efforts.
3. **At first, limit your work to those things that are out and visible.** You will tackle dresser drawers and closets after you clear those areas that are out in the open.
4. **Take a look at all the furniture in the room.** Does the room

Bedrooms

feel comfortable with the furniture it currently contains? If the room feels too crowded, identify and remove pieces of furniture until it feels more comfortable. If the room has too much clutter to determine whether or not there is too much furniture, postpone this step until later in the clutter clearing process. Removing excess furniture will make it easier to make decisions during the clutter clearing process.

5. **Is there any piece of furniture you hate or that has a negative association?** If so, remove it from the room.
6. **Remind yourself of the functions of a bedroom:** sleep, changing your clothes, and intimacy/sex. Begin identifying things in the room that don't fit those functions. Examples include: papers, project materials, computers, exercise machines, sewing machines, ironing boards, tools, bills, and professional journals.
7. **If you have many papers in the bedroom, gather them up and put them in a bag or box to be sorted later.** Place the bag or box just outside of the bedroom door.
8. **Resist the urge to read papers or sort little items on top of the dressers.** Doing that will only distract you from making significant progress on bigger items that are easier to deal with.
9. **Move other items to the door that don't fit the functions of the room,** either to just inside or just outside of the room.
10. **Don't leave the room to put away the things you are removing from the room.** As you are moving items to the doorway, sort them into the following piles: trash, donate, and move to another part of the house.
11. **Starting with the largest items in the room**—the furniture—

evaluate each item to determine if it is worthy of being in your sanctuary by repeating the mantra, "Love It, Use It, or Lose It." For each item, ask yourself these two questions: (1) do you love it for sentimental reasons or for some other type of positive association? and (2) do you use it at least once a year? If the answer is "no" on both counts, consider losing it. In other words, consider relocating it to another part of the house or donating it.

12. **Move from evaluating furniture to clothing** to shoes, books and other slightly smaller objects like CDs and DVDs.
13. **Leave small items like jewelry, coins, and medications for last.**
14. **Stop evaluating and sorting when you've accumulated so many items to be donated, relocated or taken to the trash that they trip you up, are in your way, or block the door.** Move those items out of the room to the room(s) where they belong, the trash and/or your car.
15. **Take the trash to the trash bins** so it doesn't clutter up your home.
16. **Put bags and boxes for donation directly into your car.** You won't feel the full benefit of the energy shifts resulting from clutter clearing until things are removed from your home. Resist the urge to put them anywhere else. Put them in the car.
17. **When you move items that belong in other areas of the house, do not stop and put those things away unless it is almost effortless to do so.** Plan to come back later and tidy up those spaces. Again, any stop in another room could distract you from your goal of clearing the bedroom.

Bedrooms

18. **Return to the bedroom and take a look at what you've accomplished.** Continue identifying items that don't fit the function of the space or that you no longer love or use until you are fairly certain that you've gotten most of them.
19. **Take a picture to document your progress.** Notice hot spots of clutter that remain, those places that attract your eye and bother you.
20. **Continue to clear clutter continuing to place any and all items that will leave the room by the door.** Don't leave the room.
21. **As you work your way around the room evaluating objects, begin clumping like items together, items that will be stored together.** For example, you might start with piles for dirty laundry, clothes to hang up or put away, clothes to take to the dry cleaners, shoes that will eventually be taken to the closet, books, CDs, and jewelry.
22. **Resist the urge to put clumped items away until you've finished evaluating all items.** It's instructive to be able to see how much you have of each category of items. For example, if you put things away as you work, you will miss the opportunity to get an accurate picture of just how many pairs of running shoes, pairs of black pants, ball caps, or T-shirts you own. Also, when you open drawers or enter the closet to put things away, you run the risk of being allured any chaos that calls to you from those places.
23. **If your brain shuts down and you find you are unable to make decisions about what to keep and what to pitch, check to see if you've inadvertently drifted from larger items to little stuff.** If so, shift back to larger items. If not,

take a short break and move items that have accumulated at the door.

24. **When your brain recovers, continue the process until you've covered the whole room.** This could take several sessions, depending on how much clutter there is in the room, but that's fine. You're making progress with each step. Remember, be sure to breathe deeply between each step, smile, and congratulate yourself for all you've accomplished.
25. **Take one more picture when you have finished clearing**, and compare it to your first picture. Pat yourself on your back for your hard work.

Keep in mind that this plan is written as if clutter clearing is a linear process. It is not. It can be very difficult to stay completely on track with the plan. Each plan throughout the book is meant to be a general guide, a reference point to return to when you get stuck or lose your way. If you bounce around while you're clearing and you're still getting lots done, consider it normal. If you bounce around a lot and you're not really accomplishing much, you may benefit from getting help from a supportive friend or a professional organizer.

Children's Bedrooms

Clearing Children's Toys

Toys! They come in from everywhere: birthday presents, party treat bags, Christmas gifts, McDonald's Happy Meals, in-laws, etc. They take up space. They can be difficult to store. They break, and some have small

Bedrooms

parts that seem to end up everywhere!

Arghh!!!!! Toys make extra work for busy parents, especially moms who seem to have been designated as the Toy Organizers of the Universe!

One of the best ways to stay sane when dealing with children's toys is to clear them out regularly. By doing that, you'll be teaching your children when they are young that toys are NOT meant to be permanent fixtures in your home. Toys come and go.

Birthdays and Christmas are great reminders that it's time for clearing out old toys. Any time there is a major influx of toys, take that as a toy clutter clearing opportunity. If your children are not pathological packrats, include them in the clearing as soon as they are old enough to make decisions. **If you involve children in the clearing process early on, it is much more likely that clearing their own belongings will become a habit, and the toy clearing responsibility can shift from you to them.**

Keep only those toys that fit comfortably in your child's room and in just one or two other play areas of the house. Refuse to let the toys take over every space in your home. When the space begins to feel cluttered and uncomfortable, take it as a sign that it's time to clear.

Following are seven suggestions to help you clear toy clutter:
- **Get rid of broken toys that can't be fixed.** They hold a negative energy and can attract more negativity into your life and your child's life.
- **Pitch toys that haven't been used in a year.** A year isn't a hard and fast guideline. If you know your child has lost interest in a toy after a few months, let it go!
- **Get rid of toys with many small pieces that are annoying and difficult to keep track of.** Small toy pieces are difficult

to keep up with, and when out of place become irritants.
- **Toss toys that are unwieldy or too big to store easily**, those toys you're always tripping over. That type of toy is a safety problem.
- **Get rid of toys that are worn out with the exception of a special stuffed animal or two.** Worn out items hold a tired, low energy. Their energy can affect your energy and your child's energy.
- **Pitch toys that don't work properly.** They tend not to be used because they don't work well. Also, because people usually feel frustrated that they spent money on them, those toys tend to hold the energy of frustration. Keeping up with toys can be a frustrating process. Why keep toys that are inherently frustrating?
- **Toss toys that are unsafe.** If you or your child are injured by a toy, even after you've shown him or her how to use it properly, let it go! Your child's safety is more important than any toy.

Feng Shui Challenges in Children's Rooms

Spaces that have good feng shui are peaceful and comfortable. It is seldom that I see a child's room that is peaceful. Most are loaded with a mix of toys, books, stuffed animals, furniture, and clothing. Even when everything is neatly put away, there are a lot of "conversations" going on. Conversations? Remember, everything is alive with energy, and the energy talks to you all the time. The more things you have out in the open, the more conversations there are. The smaller the things, the more

Bedrooms

energy chatter you will experience. "Too much stuff" is at the top of the list of feng shui challenges in children's rooms!

Following are some other common feng shui problems in children's rooms:

- **Too many books.** Books are high energy items. As mentioned earlier, books are made of paper, a wood element associated with growth and expansion. The words in the book are fire elements with the hot energy of fire. Since wood feeds fire, a bookshelf is the energetic equivalent of a bonfire. Do you want your child to be sleeping with a bonfire?
- **Too much little stuff out and about.** Again, as mentioned above, everything is alive with energy that talks to you. All those little hair clips, puzzle pieces, pieces of jewelry, CDs, stickers, etc., create a lot of chatter in a room meant for rest. I recommend avoiding small gifts and gifts that have a lot of small pieces. Because many children have no clue how to organize little things, I also recommend that parents help their children set up homes for all the small things they want to keep in their bedrooms, preferably out of sight in drawers or small open containers.
- **Posters with active or disturbing content.** Posters of people doing sports or singing in a concert are high energy items. Images of people are fire elements, which have the highest energy content. When people are in action, they also bring an active energy into the space that is really counter to the primary function of the room: rest. Posters with disturbing content (people in conflict, a focus on death, or themes of violence) hold negative energies that can affect the quality

of sleep. I recommend that parents set ground rules about the types of posters and pictures that are acceptable in their children's rooms, forbidding drug-and alcohol-related and violence-or death-related subjects. That would include zombies, monsters, war themes, satanic and gang-related images.

- **Too many clothes that have not been put away.** Have a 5-minute cleanup every night before bed when you work with each child to re-establish order in their room. Begin doing it with them as soon as they are capable of putting things away. Avoid doing it for them because it's easier for you and can be done more quickly. Doing that deprives your child of the opportunity to learn important maintenance skills that will serve them well when you aren't around to help out. Because many children find putting clothes away boring and annoying, without supervision they can become "droppers". If your child is a dropper, make it easier for them to keep things neat by installing hooks on the backs of doors and providing bins or baskets to catch clothes.

Help your child make their room a peaceful personal paradise. It will help them sleep better and have more mental clarity for good decision-making.

Create Good Feng Shui in Children's Rooms

When children are young, you have more ability to affect the feng shui of their bedrooms because they are more likely accept your direction and ideas. Once children get old enough to have specific desires about how they want their room to look, it's more important that they be able to express themselves in their room . . . within limits, than that their rooms have optimal feng shui. Personal expression empowers them and helps them figure out who they are and what is important to them. Therefore, the suggestions I offer here are for creating good feng shui in the early years of your children's lives.

As I've already mentioned, I highly recommend you make it clear that anything with violent, satanic, or drug-and alcohol-related content or inferences is prohibited. The energies of those types of things are extremely toxic and are not the kind of subconscious programming you want your child to be exposed to for eight or more hours per night, plus any daytime hours spent in the space.

I also recommend you have guidelines regarding food and cleaning up after eating. Otherwise, your child could create some nasty feng shui when the food and crumbs attract bugs.

You can create and maintain good feng shui in children's rooms by taking the following steps:

- **Put color on the walls.** Avoid white walls that tend to become dingy and scuffed more quickly than walls that have color. White walls are also associated with anxiety and depression, like the gray skies in winter that are associated with Seasonal Affective Disorder (SAD). The luscious colors in children's art and posters won't show up as well on white walls as they will on walls that are painted a color.
- **Avoid using red, bright yellow, or a vibrant shade of any color,** on bedroom walls. Color is energy; therefore, your child will sleep better in a room painted with a restful color

(shades of blue, green, sand, cool purple, buttery yellow), not a high-energy color.

- **Use vibrant colors in small touches** in bedding patterns, art, window coverings, rugs, and toys. Vibrant colors in small doses can give the room a nice moderate energy without being overwhelming and affecting sleep.
- **Remove books to a shelf or bookcase** in the playroom, family room, or home office. Books are high energy items, and children can be affected by their content while sleeping. It's preferable to allow only a few books at a time into the room, and store the bulk of them in another location.
- **Store high energy items** like toys, arts and craft supplies, and electronic devices out of sight in bins, drawers, closets, cabinets or outside of the bedroom. They have a noisy energy that can detract from the overall feng shui of the room and can make the place feel like a bustling busy street instead of a place of rest.
- **Contain small objects in bins or rolling drawers.** Small items that are left out in plain sight are alive with a busy, noisy energy that does not complement the primary function of a child's bedroom; rest.
- **Be open to removing the student desk and homework/studying items** from the room, especially if your child prefers to study in places other than his/her bedroom. From a feng shui perspective, it is preferable that school work be done in another location and that the bedroom activities be limited to sleep, changing clothes, pleasure reading, and quietly playing with toys. Studying, school books and school assignments are work and are associated with performance,

therefore they usually create some level of anxiety and stress. The content of books, notebooks, and assignments, and the feelings associated with them, are not conducive to good sleep.

- **Have wall hangings with relevant, positive associations.** As soon as your children have opinions about what matters to them, let them choose the posters, prints, and photographs that adorn their bedroom walls, within the limits suggested above. Art is a way children can express and inspire themselves. Guide your children to choose art with subjects that will remind them of who they are and what is really important in their lives.
- **Teach your children to keep their rooms neat and organized at a young age,** so they will develop the habit of maintaining a peaceful bedroom. Make picking up their room a daily maintenance activity when they are young, so that by the time they hit the busyness of upper grades, keeping their rooms neat will be automatic instead of an annoying "have-to" imposed by Mom.

Teach Children to Live Clutter-Free

Having a child who always chooses to live neatly is probably a dream, given the complexity of children's lives these days. However, you do have influence over your children and can begin teaching them how to be conscious of their belongings and the impact they have on themselves, your home and family.

- **Consider giving children gift cards to their favorite establishments** instead of lots of little gifts that never get used, just so they will have packages to open at Christmas and on other holidays. Instead of giving gift cards to get more stuff, give them cards to their favorite eating establishments or for activities they would enjoy, like membership to the zoo or to a museum, or tickets for a play or for a special excursion to a place they have always wanted to visit. This type of gift sends the message that experiences, and activities are a way to get pleasure, de-emphasizing the significance of things that can clutter up a space.
- **Model clutter clearing at every opportunity.** Make sure they see you managing clutter every day, witness you clearing your closet seasonally, and clearing whenever there is a new influx of things at holidays and on birthdays. Your actions speak much louder than your words.
- **Teach them the "Love It, Use It, or Lose It Method" of clutter clearing.** Items that are worthy of keeping in the prime real estate of their rooms are things they love or use at least once a year. Encourage them to give away or throw away (Lose It!) any things that they don't love or use.
- **Involve your child in daily clutter clearing.** For instance, urge them to recycle school papers that are no longer useful, put recycling bins outside for pickup, move items to other parts of the house when you are clearing counters and living spaces, and help you pick up rooms during your daily clutter clearing activities.
- **Schedule a daily clean-up time.** Set a timer for five to ten minutes every evening before bedtime and have everyone

Bedrooms

use that time to put things away, take dishes to the sink, and create order in both the public areas of the home as well as in the bedrooms. Start doing this when children are very young (4 or 5), but old enough to put their toys away. That way it will become a habit to clean up every day instead of relying on Mom to do clutter clearing for them. The longer you wait to enlist their help, the more likely it is that they will resist doing their part in household clutter clearing. By the time they are in middle school they will have been trained to think, "Why do I have to help? Isn't that Mom's job?"

- **Schedule a major clutter clearing session with each child once or twice a year.** The summer is a great time to do this, letting go of old notebooks and papers from the previous school year in preparation for the new year. It will also teach them that when you finish one chapter of your life, it's beneficial to clear the old before launching into the new. Pre- or post-Christmas and birthdays are also good times to initiate a major clearing session, since there will be new toys, books, clothes and other items coming into their rooms.

- **Teach your child to clear clutter for good:** their own good, the good of the family, and the good of their community. When they clear things they no longer love or use, they will have more mental clarity, make better decisions, and make space for more of what they really want in life. Their clearing will have a positive effect on the whole house, because everything is connected, and clutter can cause irritation and conflict among family members. What they clear and donate to charities can become a blessing to people in the community. A pre-Christmas clearing can be a great community service project for a family, as it will make space for gifts received and will teach children that some children don't have so many nice toys and books as they have and will benefit from receiving some of their toys, books, etc.

When clutter clearing becomes a part of daily life for your children, you'll have fewer clutter problems. Your children will be less stressed and better equipped to deal with the many challenges of growing into responsible, productive adults.

Sleep: The Primary Function of Children's Bedrooms

The common functions of children's rooms are: rest, play, study and dressing. As you can see, three of those functions are active functions. Having an abundance of items in the room that are associated with activities like play (toys, books), study (school books, school supplies, computers) and dressing (clothes, shoes, jewelry, etc.) can have a significant effect on the quality of a child's sleep. Then, if you add other high energy things like TVs, video games, sewing machines, craft and art supplies, electronic equipment, videos, CDs, and clutter, the room can feel like a roaring crowd, full of noise and distractions.

I've probably got you thinking, "What can I do about all that noise, so my child can sleep peacefully?"

Below are changes that can make your child's bedroom a place of rest:
- **Consider removing the study function of the room to another part of the house** unless your children really prefer

Bedrooms

to study in their room. If you move the study area, choose an active area on the first floor. Dining rooms that are seldom used for dining can be set up as a place to study by using an armoire to house the computer, papers, books and school supplies.

- **Keep only those toys in the bedroom that involve a quiet kind of play,** like dolls and stuffed animals.
- **Remove electronic games, TVs and computers from the room.** Those items are very high energy and put off electromagnetic energy that can interfere with sleep.
- **Remove games to the family room or playroom**, especially those that require a lot of mental energy.
- **Remove books to the home office, playroom or family room.** Books are high energy objects, and your children are affected by the content of those books while sleeping. If your child likes to read or you like to read to him/her before bed, bring in a book or two to enjoy. When finished with them, return them to book shelves in other parts of the house.
- **Teach your child the habit of putting dirty clothes in a hamper and putting away clothes and shoes in his/her closet or drawers on a daily basis.** You may have to do this with them nightly until they know where everything goes, and it becomes a habit, particularly with younger children. Some children have brain wiring challenges like ADHD that make putting things away very difficult. If that is the case, work with your child for five minutes every night to restore order in their room. Make it "talk time" with Mom or Dad, a time to connect while working together, not an odious chore.

Remember that a lack of sleep or poor-quality sleep affects every area of a child's life. To ensure that your child is able to function well in cognitive and emotional arenas, make the sleep function the primary focus of your child's bedroom.

Moms, Let Kids Get Rid of Belongings

When I work with moms and their children to help clear clutter and organize children's rooms and play areas, I often find that a child is ready to part with an item, but Mom is not. I remember a client I worked with whose young daughter knew what she wanted and what she no longer wanted to have in her space. Her mother, on the other hand, was a sentimental saver who had great difficulty parting with things. I knew I would likely have a challenge on my hands if we all worked together.

I've been in that situation before. Typically, the child will identify something to donate to a charity and the mother will say, "Oh, your stuffed penguin, are you sure you want to get rid of that?" At that point, I usually intervene and say, "If she wants to get rid of it, let her. If it means that much to you, you keep it for yourself." Inside I'm saying, "It's a good thing that she wants to get rid of things. Don't discourage that!"

Fortunately, I'd worked with this client before and had prepared her for our session by encouraging her to let me work with her daughter by myself. I assuaged her fears that we might get rid of things that she thought should be kept by letting her know we'd show her what we planned to get rid of. Working alone with the daughter, we were able to fill three large garbage bags of toys and craft items to donate and two bags of trash.

My client was so thrilled by our progress that she even allowed us

Bedrooms

to close two of the bags without checking to see what was going out of the house. I am fairly certain we'd have been much less successful if Mom had been involved. Her second guessing her daughter's decisions would have slowed our progress and would have led to the daughter to feeling discouraged, angry, or even disempowered. Getting Mom out of the picture was a win-win for both mother and daughter. The child was given the chance to make her own decisions, with me monitoring the process, and Mom was able to get part of her house cleared out without the usual angst and agony.

Moms, if your children want to get rid of their belongings, let them! Don't second guess their decisions! If you truly think they are making a mistake, put the item or items aside with things you want to keep for yourself. When you second guess their decisions, you are teaching them that they really can't make good decisions on their own behalf. You are also teaching them to save instead of purge! Do you really want that?

From Cluttered to Clear in Just One Year

Children's Rooms Clutter Clearing Plan

Until children are able to make decisions, mothers typically clear their children's rooms for them. Even when children are capable of making decisions, don't assume that they know how to clear clutter from their rooms or even how to keep their rooms clean and organized. Initially it is advisable for mothers to work with their children to teach them how to make decisions about what to keep and what to get rid of, how to clear things in an organized fashion, and how to move items from their room to appropriate locations; by the outside door for donations, to the trash, or to other parts of the house (not to your bedroom, the hall, the attic, etc.). Moms who don't teach their children how to clear and what to do with cleared items are more likely to find purged items dumped in other parts of the house, even in the master bedroom.

By the time children reach adolescence, many of them prefer to clear their belongings on their own and just need to be reminded to do it on a regular basis.

1. **Take a photograph of the room before starting to clear it.** Look at the photo and take note of the hot spots, those areas that make you want to run from the room. You'll want to be sure to address them, even though their energy is anything but inviting!
2. **Since the primary function of a child's room is a place to sleep**, set your intention to establish a space that will be conducive to restful sleep and quiet activities.
3. **If there is paper in the room, gather it into bags or boxes** and put them aside until the end of the clearing process. If you start with paper, you will see and feel significant progress

quickly and are likely to quit.

4. **Quiet the noisy energy of small things** in the room by gathering them into baskets, bags or boxes. Set them aside to be dealt with at the end of the clearing process. Gathering up paper and small items creates an immediate sense of order, gives you a feeling of accomplishment, and makes it easier to make decisions.

5. **Check out the furniture in the room.** Is it still appropriate given the age of the child? Is it still in good condition? Remove any furniture that no longer is appropriate, useful, or in good condition. Items that could be removed are student desks or bookshelves. Both are associated with either work (studying) or high energy objects (books), things whose energy will interfere with restful sleep.

6. **Then start sorting <u>big</u> items like toys, games, clothing or books, whichever category is easiest for you and your child to deal with.** Determine if each item will be kept, trashed, donated or given away to a specific person.

7. **Divide items** to be kept into 1) those that will remain in the bedroom and 2) those that will be relocated to other areas of the house. Put items that will go to other parts of the house outside the bedroom door in one pile.

8. **For toys and books, identify items that are no longer age-appropriate** and donate or trash them if they are not in good condition. Encourage your child to let go of things he/she no longer uses by reminding them that he/she can make a difference in the life of another child who isn't fortunate to have nice things by donating his/her things to a local charity.

9. **Check the sizes of clothing and donate or trash** clothing

that no longer fits or is no longer in good condition. Be sure to throw away clothing that is too worn to be donated.

10. **Put toys, books, and clothing** that will be donated in a second pile outside of the bedroom door.
11. **Remove the bulk of the remaining books** that are still age appropriate for the child to be taken to another location, perhaps a playroom or family room. Books are high energy items that can interfere with sleep.
12. **Remove games from the room to be taken to the family room**. Games have an active energy that is counter to the primary function of the bedroom: rest.
13. **Check out the content of art and wall hangings**. Are they still age appropriate? Is the content appropriate for a child's room? Is it in good condition? Remove any art/wall hangings that your child has outgrown, that is no longer of interest to your child, or that is faded or torn.
14. **Remove the bulk of arts and craft supplies** from the room to be taken to the area of the house where they will be used. Leave a few coloring books, colored pencils and art pads in the room if your child enjoys drawing in the quiet of his/her room.
15. **When the largest items in the room** have been sorted and moved to their appropriate locations in the bedroom or out of the bedroom, sort the small items by category (jewelry, small toys, coins, puzzle pieces, toy pieces, etc.). As you sort pull out items that can be thrown away or donated. Move those items to the trash or your donation pile.
16. **When everything in the room has been sorted and evaluated, review the paper that was gathered up at the**

beginning of the organizing process. Keep only those papers that will be referenced again, that hold special significance, like a good grade that your child is especially proud of, or that are interesting examples of your child's writing.

17. **Put papers that are considered memorabilia,** documenting your child's accomplishments or writing abilities, into one large plastic bin and store it on the bottom of your child's closet, if there is sufficient room. If the box doesn't fit in the bedroom, choose another easy-to-access location.

18. **Papers that are kept because they will be referenced again while studying or reviewing for testing should be stored in the study area outside the bedroom.** If they are kept in the bedroom they should be stored out of sight in a book bag or a drawer.

19. **Remove items that will go to other parts of the house to their new locations.** Do not stop to put them away. Make a mental note to put them away after you finish working in your child's bedroom.

20. **Remove items to be donated and place them in your car** to be dropped off at the charity of your choice.

21. **Take trash bags** to the trash can.

22. **Once you have cleared out everything that is no longer loved or used**, create a new order of the things that remain. It will be much easier to do so when there are far fewer items in the room.

23. **Take a photograph of the room and celebrate** your accomplishment.

From Cluttered to Clear in Just One Year

Your child's room is a work in progress, changing as your child grows and changes. Remember that the primary function of the room is as a peaceful haven for sleep. The negative energy of clutter or too much stuff is not restful. Make sure that clutter clearing happens often enough to ensure that the room stays peaceful and uncluttered.

CHAPTER 3

Kitchen

"The kitchen really is the castle itself. This is where we spend our happiest moments and where we find the joy of being a family."
—Mario Batali

The kitchen is the heart of a home. It's the gathering spot for all family members. It's where people go for nourishment and connection with other family members. The kitchen is a public room that usually has a much higher energy than other public rooms in the house, because there is so much more activity in that space than in other rooms.

Because the kitchen is a high traffic area, it often becomes a drop spot for papers and items that belong in other parts of the house. It also houses multiple functions: meal preparation, eating, interacting with other family members, household organizing activities (meal planning, processing school papers for children, managing the family calendar, etc.). Whenever a room has multiple purposes, it is more challenging to organize and keep clutter free.

Women tend to center out of the kitchen because they often coordinate activities that occur in a kitchen and in the home. Working from the kitchen, the heart of the home, gives them easy access to other family members. A clutter-free and well-organized kitchen promotes feeling grounded and in control, and allows women to more easily juggle all the responsibilities that come with being a wife and mother.

Kitchen Clutter Clearing: <u>How</u> to Start

I'll bet that when you think about clearing clutter in your kitchen you immediately feel somewhat overwhelmed. That is a normal response, given the complexity of this important space. Try to remember that your kitchen is the *heart* of your home, so your efforts will help create a space to *fuel your heart.*

Why Do You Feel Overwhelmed?

A kitchen is a complex area housing a large number of items. Many of us handle that quantity and complexity by creating multiple regions in the space to house mass quantities of items, like the pantry or "junk drawer." Therefore, my first suggestion is that you NOT plan to clear your whole kitchen in one clutter clearing session. Rather, break it down by region, starting with one that will be:

- The **easiest** to tackle
- The one housing the **greatest number of things that can be tossed or given away**
- The one with the **largest objects**

Kitchen

Start in Regions Where You Have Large Objects

It's important to make significant progress quickly. If you don't make progress quickly you're likely to feel overwhelmed and/or discouraged and quit. The categories above are likely to give you the most bang for your time and energy bucks! Often, a good place to start is where you have the most storage.

I usually start clearing clutter in clients' kitchens either in the pantry/food storage area (because I can often find expired foods to pitch in the trash), the appliance area, or where pots and pans are stored. The pots and pans area is a great place to find duplicates. Which skillets do you actually use? Which never get used? Decisions to let go of things are easier to make when you know you have other objects of the same type.

The appliance area and the pots and pans area are two regions that usually hold the largest items in the kitchen. When you begin in a region where you're able to move large objects out of the room, the energy in the space will immediately shift; the bigger the objects, the bigger the shift. For example, deciding to get rid of an old mixer, one that you rarely use or that never worked well in the first place, will give you a feeling of accomplishment, compared to how you'd feel if you got rid of a several small containers of spices.

It's the energy shift that keeps you moving. When you start to see space where none existed before, the energy shift will lift your spirits. When you feel that rush of energy from your clutter clearing accomplishment, you'll want to feel more of that good feeling. So, you're more likely to keep going.

Work from Region to Region

I recommend you work your way from region to region. In each region work from biggest items to smallest, from easiest to tackle to hardest. If you find yourself shutting down, stop and ask yourself, "Am I doing the easiest first? Am I doing the biggest things first?" Overwhelm typically happens when you've drifted to smaller items or your brain is just too tired to continue. Making decisions is hard work!

Kitchen Clutter Clearing: Where to Start

As I'm considering where to start clearing kitchens with clients, I not only consider where I'll find the largest items, the easiest things to clear, and where I'll find the most things that can be purged, I also try to determine where I'm most likely to find the most "dead" stuff. Dead stuff are items about which I'll get no objection when I suggest purging them. "Dead" means no energy, nothing appealing, no need to keep. It usually feels good to get rid of dead stuff.

Often the prime dead stuff location in a kitchen is a choice between foodstuffs that have been around since the Ice Age or the bottom or top shelves of a cabinet that hold miscellaneous occasional use items in disarray. Of course, the bigger the items, the better! Recently when choosing where to start I got my answer when I opened the pantry door. The shelves were about three feet deep. Because the back of each shelf was difficult to see or reach I knew there would be lots of dead items hiding in the darkness, especially on the upper shelves.

Sure enough, from the back end of those shelves I unearthed many items that would be risky to eat. In some cases, expiration dates helped make the decision. In other cases, my client took one look at the long-lost item and exclaimed, "Oh, throw that away!"

When clearing any area, your first goal is to quickly get things moving out. When items start flowing toward the trash or the donation pile, you will feel energized. And, you'll need that energy to keep going through all the many types of items that get housed in a kitchen!

Whose Kitchen Is It Anyway?

Whose kitchen are you working in? Does your kitchen reflect the kind of cook you are, the kind of cook you once were, or the kind of cook you hope to be? Ideally, you want your kitchen to reflect who you are today. In other words, it should contain only those items that you use with some regularity, not those you once used or those you might use someday when the stars are aligned properly, and you suddenly have oodles of time to do gourmet cooking.

Energy from the Past

In order to keep vibrant energy in the kitchen (and in your heart), you want the energy of this room to reflect where you are in your life at this moment. Not the past. Not the future. Keeping kitchen tools and equipment that you no longer use, and are unlikely to use in the future, holds the energy of the past in place. They also often anchor nostalgic feelings and sadness that things have changed. Stocking up on items that you might use, but never do, keeps you yearning for more time to cook and perhaps even resenting your current reality that doesn't allow for the pleasure of spending more time in the kitchen.

Release Energy of the Past by Letting Go

Trust that if you have a change of heart or a change of schedule, you will be able to purchase replacements for anything you purge. I let go of round cake pans, because no matter how hard I tried, I could never make a round cake that wasn't lopsided. I have never regretted that decision. Sheet cakes taste just as good as round cakes! I also got rid of my bundt pan, because I never made that type of cake. Recently when I found a recipe that I really wanted to try, one that called for a bundt pan, I was able to pick one up at low cost at the grocery store.

Energy of the Present

Modify your kitchen so that it's an accurate reflection of your current eating habits and abilities. When you get real about your commitment to cooking or lack thereof, I predict you'll feel more comfortable in your kitchen. Its cabinets and drawers will be telling the truth about how the space is actually used.

When Abundance Is Not Good Feng Shui

One of my favorite places to start clutter clearing in a kitchen is with canned goods and processed foods in the pantry. I almost always find expired foods there. They usually go out of date for one of two reasons: 1) they hide out at the back of a deep shelf, unseen by those in search of food to use for a meal; 2) they are part of an enormous jumble of food stuffs in the kitchen of a person who buys in bulk and therefore are not visible.

The trick to remedying both situations is to make all food stuffs visible. In the first situation, it's better to avoid putting smaller items behind larger ones. This can be accomplished in several ways. You can put tall, bulky items at the back of deep shelves with smaller items in front. Or, if you have a number of identical items, you can line them from the front to the back of a shelf. That way the first item you see will tell you what's also at the back of the shelf. Be sure to arrange items on the shelf so that those that expire first are close to the front of the line. A third option is to use a plastic kitchen product that looks like bleachers. I found one at *Bed Bath and Beyond*, called the Copco Non-Skid 15-Inch Shelf Organizer. This product is particularly good for cans because it raises each line of cans a bit higher than the previous, high enough to be able to identify the contents. This type of organizer is also available in other sizes to accommodate both smaller and larger items.

The more quantity you have in a pantry or food storage areas, the more challenging it is to keep things organized for full visibility, and the more likely that some food will expire before being used. Consider limiting bulk purchases to only those items you use quickly. Resist the urge to restock your shelves until you know exactly what you already have and actually need.

Recently a client and I had a good laugh over the quantities of canned tomato products and beans we found in her pantry. She just kept buying tomatoes and beans because she eats them often and didn't want to run out. Little did she know that her deep shelves were already well-stocked! She just hadn't been able to see all of the products at a glance.

Make it your goal to avoid wasting food by working hard to keep all food visible, and by resisting the urge to buy in bulk when you aren't certain what food you actually need. Keeping food stores organized and visible will also make meal planning easier!

Want Peace in the Family? Clear Kitchen Countertops!

At this time of kitchen gadgets and appliances galore, it's not uncommon to find kitchen counters clogged with those "essentials." I challenge you to do a survey of those items asking yourself, "How often do I use this?"

I'll bet you can cut those "essentials" in half if you limit countertop items to those you use every day. Any item used less often can be stored in a cabinet, pantry or even a garage overflow storage area, and retrieved when needed.

The energy of the items displayed on your counters talks to you and everyone else in the kitchen. Multiple appliances and gadgets create lots of energy chatter. Lots of chatter can become lots of stress, particularly when you add the chatter of family members to the mix. Remove the chatter by removing those items, and you'll find that your kitchen feels much more peaceful.

It's also difficult to make cluttered countertops look attractive. "Attractive? Kitchens are meant to be functional, not necessarily attractive," you say. I say, "Why not functional AND attractive?" Treat your kitchen as a 3D collage of those things that bring family and friends together, and you'll find interactions with others in that space not only more harmonious, but also more connected. Environment affects performance. A cluttered space tends to irritate the nervous system. A lovely space soothes it. Which would you prefer?

Kitchen Clutter: Reducing Duplicates

The kitchen is one area of the house where I find the greatest quantity of duplicates. Perhaps it's because people combine households when they marry or move in together, both bringing all the necessary kitchen equipment. Or, new couples may be reluctant to get rid of any of their kitchen items because they might need them if the relationship ends. Perhaps some believe their kitchen equipment is superior to that of their partner. I suspect that the most common reason for duplicates when

Kitchen

couples move in together is that, in the stress and time crunch of moving in, making decisions about what to keep and what to pitch is more than they have the brain power to deal with at that stressful time. In the moment it seems easier to throw everything together and plan to make those tough decisions later. Unfortunately, later never comes!

Another common reason for duplicates is that a newer model of appliance or kitchen tool comes out and is purchased, yet people don't always dispose of the older model. Perhaps they want to make sure the new one is actually superior to the old one. Or, they think there could be a time when they might need both of them. Again, another decision is pushed to the side in the busyness of life. After all, what's the big deal if you have four potato peelers and two blenders?

Whatever the reason for duplicates, eliminating duplicate items that are not used is another great place to begin kitchen clutter clearing. Take your kitchen section by section and look for duplicates. For example, take a look at all your mixing bowls. You are sure to have your favorites, the ones you reach for every time. If you have two bowls of the same size, get rid of the one that though useful, you never use.

You can even look for duplicates in your spice area. It's helpful to group your spices in two categories: main meal and baking. When you do that, it's easy to see that you have three nutmeg containers and two of cilantro. Eliminate the older containers, keeping only those that you think are still potent.

When you streamline your kitchen, keeping only those items that you actually use, keeping the best of all your tools and ingredients, you will release quantities of stagnant, negative energy. You will also reduce stress, because it will be so much easier to access anything you need to prepare meals. When you shift negative energies to positive by getting real about what you actually use on a daily basis, you might find you are more willing to step out of your comfort zone and try a new recipe!

Cookbook Clutter: Let Go of the Fantasy

Almost without fail, I find at least twice as many cookbooks per household than each family actually uses. In this age of fast food and take-out dinners, why do so many women hold on to volumes and volumes of cookbooks? Yes, there's always the fall back excuse of, "I might need it someday, when I finally figure out how to find time for cooking in addition to raising two children and being the CEO of our home."

But, I wonder if in fact those cookbooks hold the energy of an old fantasy many women carry, about being able to enjoy the search for the perfect recipe to round out a luscious meal that they lovingly prepare for their family. The frenetic pace of life with the burgeoning demands on a woman's time have literally robbed women of the time and space to thoughtfully prepare meals for their family.

Meal preparation can be a comforting, loving act, supported by helpful recipes for every kind of food. However, congested schedules and an ever-increasing focus on activity at the cost of relationships have shifted the focus of many families away from the benefits of a nightly pause to enjoy a meal. Too often families are just grabbing calories to be able to keep going. Unless a family can afford a housekeeper, thoughtful meal preparation is too often limited to special occasions like birthdays, holidays, and perhaps an occasional weekend meal.

So Why All the Cookbooks?

I believe many women still want what once was possible before this age of technology, with its excessive doing and super-fast everything—to be able cook for their family on a regular basis. Perhaps the cookbooks hold the energy of a time when enjoying meal preparation was possible. They offer hope that meal preparation can matter again.

As such, cookbooks also hold a nostalgic, sad energy. Keeping many more cookbooks than you ever touch in one year only holds that sadness in place. Excessive cookbooks can also hold an accusing type of energy. Their subtle message is that somehow you are not getting it right, because you can't figure out how to make use of those valuable resources with all that you have going on. They can be a physical reminder, telling you that you are not the best wife and mother that you could be. And, guess what? They are lying!

The truth of the matter is that our world has changed. Ideally your kitchen and its contents should change as well. Start by clearing out cookbooks you've NEVER used, despite their lovely photos. Keep only one good reference cookbook plus those specialty cookbooks that contain recipes that you actually prepare or that have recipes for the types of food you actually do have time to prepare. Remember, if you by chance let go of a cookbook you later need, recipes are available **everywhere**: in magazines, on the internet, from friends and family members, in gift stores, and in bookstores. There is no chance that you will ever starve from lack of a specific recipe!

Make it your mission to have your cookbooks reflect your current reality. Acknowledge the sadness of the unrealized fantasy and the loss of a more peaceful way of life. You can create a new reality that includes those precious recipes that actually get used when you are able to make time to nurture yourself and your family with thoughtful meal preparation.

The "Junk" Drawer: The Mini-Attic in the Kitchen

Don't know what to do with the curtains you removed from a child's bedroom? Stick them in the attic! Don't know what to do with miscellaneous pieces of plastic that might be important for some reason? Stick them in the junk drawer! Is it any wonder that most people cringe, not only when attics are mentioned, but also when junk drawers become the subject of conversation? Junk drawers are the "I don't know what to do with it" places for small items, often located in the kitchen.

What I don't understand is how that drawer of miscellaneous items got its name. Often most of the things in a junk drawer are not junk. They are useful items: screw drivers and other small tools, pencils, pens, batteries, nail files, sewing kits, screws and nails, gum, rubber bands . . . I'll bet junk drawers were so named because their contents were jumbled and <u>looked</u> junky!

I object to using the adjective "junk" to describe any storage area in a house, because using "junk" to describe a space gives it permission to be junky. I once had a client who had a junk room! Can you imagine giving over one whole room in a house to junk?!

Believe it or not, junk drawers can be transformed from junky spaces to organized places with organizer inserts or small containers to hold the different categories of things you choose to keep in that drawer. You can even find those containers around the house. Small jewelry boxes check boxes, and small plastic food containers work well in a junk drawer. Both lids and boxes can be used.

Be sure to limit the contents of each container to one category. For example, one container might hold batteries, another would hold pens and pencils, and a third would hold miscellaneous tools. Don't mix items within a container or you'll transform your neatly organized drawer of miscellaneous small items back into a junk drawer.

If you want to be successful at maintaining a really useful storage space for miscellaneous small things in your kitchen, let go of the "junk drawer" label. Call your newly organized drawer of miscellaneous small items something fun like the Picasso drawer or the Discovery drawer. You'll be glad you did the next time you are able to quickly find that miscellaneous piece of plastic that turns out to be the battery cover for the back of your TV remote!

Counter Knife Blocks: A Feng Shui Kitchen No-No!

One of the most common feng shui errors that I find in kitchens is the presence of a knife block on the counter. You know, a block of wood holding knives of various sizes. It's a very convenient way to store knives so they are easily accessible for use. However, when assessing the feng shui of a space, it's important to consider safety. Knives are not only kitchen tools, they can also be used as weapons. Knives that are located out in the open in a knife block are not considered safe because they are weapons that are easily accessible. A block of knives is a block of negative energy because of its potential for harm.

You are probably thinking, "If I can't store them on the counter, how should I store them for easy access?" You have several options. First, you may be able to make room on a shelf in one of your lower cabinets for the knife block. Make sure you don't have to bend very far to grab a knife. If it's the least bit inconvenient, you will avoid accessing knives. Then the block will either end up on the counter again, or the knives will be left out on the counter or tossed into drawers.

A second option, and my preferred option, is to purchase a wooden drawer insert specifically for knives. Make sure you measure the drawer first, so you are sure to buy an insert of the correct size. The insert will have slits to hold the knives, safely containing the blades out of harm's way.

Removing a knife block from the counter is a great way to make a kitchen immediately feel more peaceful. Commit to peace and safety in your kitchen by removing your knife block from the counter.

Ten Steps to Clutter Clearing Your Kitchen Desk

The kitchen is the heart of the home. It is often a hub where family members gather for nurturance and communing with each other. As mentioned earlier, the kitchen is often where women center their energy. As such, it has become an action area, not only for food preparation, but for women to coordinate a variety of activities as diverse as meal planning, scheduling appointments, coordinating schedules, and making important phone calls.

The kitchen desk probably came into being to accommodate the ever-increasing needs of women to have an office of sorts close to where they spend most of their time. The idea was good, creating an area for the CEO of the home to work. I know, you're already laughing! Who works at their kitchen desk? Who even sits in front of a kitchen desk?

First of all, kitchen desks are usually about the size of a postage stamp—too small to accommodate the needs of a busy family. Also, they are not comfortable places to sit because they are built-in pieces of furniture which force you to sit facing a wall with your back to the rest of the room. Sitting with your back to a room puts your nervous system

Kitchen

on high alert, ready for any possible threat. In that state, it's difficult to focus. Consequently, the chairs of those desks, if they even exist, are rarely used, except as a stacking spot for paper and other objects.

Kitchen desks of even the most organized women quickly become drop spots. Typical desk clutter consists of papers that come in from children returning from school, the mailbox, and meetings, plus all kinds of other objects that family members drop on their travels through the kitchen. Most people just roll their eyes when they look at their kitchen desk. Unless properly set up and managed, it is often a source of frustration, as well as an eyesore.

Clearing clutter from a kitchen desk first involves separating papers from other objects.

Work with objects first:
- **Sort objects** into those that belong in the kitchen and those that do not.
- **As you're sorting, feel free to pitch any items** you know you don't need, love, or that aren't worth the effort of moving to another location.
- **Put items that belong elsewhere** just outside the kitchen door to be dispersed to their appropriate homes <u>after</u> you finish working on the desk.
- **Put away those items that do belong in the kitchen.** That may involve going into drawers associated with the desk. Resist the urge to organize the drawers at this time. Your first focus is on restoring order to the desk top.
- **If objects don't fit in a drawer, put them aside** to deal with when you clear out the drawers.

Once you've addressed the objects on the desk top, sort the papers that were on the desk.
- **Pull out the biggest chunks first:** the newsletters, magazines, and stapled-together papers
- **Toss or recycle those that are no longer relevant.**
- **Sort the remaining papers into the following categories:**
    - **Trash** (recycling)
    - **Refer Out** (goes to another location or person)
    - **Action** (separate papers associated with actions to be taken at this location from actions to be taken outside the kitchen)
    - **Reference** (e.g. contacts, schedules)
    - **Filing** (separate papers that will be filed at this location from those that will be filed elsewhere)
    - **Pending** (e.g. tickets for an event, directions to a social event, etc.)
    - **Reading** (optional reading)
    - **Possibilities** (e.g. information about products that you could use or events that you might attend)

The only papers that should remain on the desk are the action papers. The desktop is an action area. It ceases to be an action area when clogged with papers that need filing, reading, or are references and possibilities.

Next, move papers to their appropriate locations.
- **Move papers associated with actions** that will be taken outside of the kitchen to the area where the action will take place.

Kitchen

- **Move paper to be filed** outside of the kitchen to the area where it will be filed.
- **Move reading papers** to an area where they are most likely to be read.
- **If you have already set up files, file papers immediately** up receipt.
- **Store reference items** in files or binders.
- **Put possibilities** in a paper tray or file that can be easily accessed.

A good filing solution for the kitchen is an open filing box for files to accommodate all the types of paper you need to access from the kitchen. It could be stored on the counter, but preferably under the counter in a cabinet or in the opening where the chair slips under the counter. It must be easy to access so frequent filing is easy to do.

Whew! Who knew that clearing clutter from a kitchen desk could be so complicated? Anywhere you have paper, you have complexity. When you set up a system for managing paper you need to access in the kitchen, and you use it faithfully, maintaining order on the kitchen desk gets easier.

Remember, keep only those things at the kitchen desk that you regularly use in the kitchen. I call those tiny desk areas "prime real estate." If you want to maximize the potential of a kitchen desk, you can't afford to park useless things on those small surfaces. If kept clear and set up properly, they can function as the cockpit for the coordination of most of the activities of a busy family. Is that how your kitchen desk functions? If not, why not? Claim your kitchen desk as a mini-home office, an action area at the heart of the home.

From Cluttered to Clear in Just One Year

Kitchen Clutter Clearing Plan

Following is a recommended order for clearing your kitchen. This is just a recommendation. You'll notice I've chosen to start with areas that house large items with no great complexity and finish with areas of great complexity. This list is meant to be a guide. As you clear, you are likely to find yourself naturally drifting to the next best area for you to clear. Go with that inclination unless it leads you to the complicated little stuff.

Appliances	Condiment area
Pots & pans	Dish towels and pot holders
Baking pans	Silverware drawer
Mixing bowls	Kitchen tool drawer
Dishes, glasses, mugs	Spices
Coffee area	Junk drawer
Cookbooks & recipes	Kitchen desk
Food storage containers	Miscellaneous occasional use items
Pantry	
Cleaning products	

1. **Identify the first region you will tackle.** Make sure it contains large items, lots of items that can be trashed or donated or is super easy to clear. Set up bags for trash and donation.
2. **Evaluate each item.** Be truthful and ruthless! Do you use it at least once a year? Do you have more than one of this type of item? Is it easy to use or is it annoying? If it's annoying, consider getting rid of it. If it's a food item, is it still edible? Is

Kitchen

it a type of food you still enjoy eating?

3. **Compare duplicates.** When you find duplicates, identify the item(s) that works best, the one(s) that you regularly choose to use. Keep the best and get rid of the rest. Donate the duplicates that still work well. Trash the others. If you have duplicates of spices, keep the freshest and toss the older containers.
4. **Reorganize.** Once you've cleared out items that you don't use, reorganize the items that are left.
5. **Add containers to hold small items** that tend to float on a shelf or get lost at the back of cabinets.
6. **Strive to make all items visible.** Keep smaller items at the front of shelves and larger items at the back. Store occasional use items on higher shelves and most used items at a level between your shoulder and your hip.

When you finish one region, move on to the next on the list. Continue from region to region until the kitchen is done.

As you work, be open to new ideas coming to you for rearranging regions or sections within regions. Once you clear some of the clutter, you may realize that there is a better way to organize your kitchen given how you currently work in it.

As you work through your kitchen, resist the urge to drift to other areas of the house, and definitely do not get hung up on doing the job perfectly. Your goal is to lighten your load by examining each region, identifying those items you use less than once a year, broken items, items you hate, items that don't work well, duplicate items and items that are not safe to eat.

Remember, the kitchen is the heart of the home. A clear and organized "heart" makes the everyday activities of meal preparation and communing with family members a pleasure that can feed your heart and soul.

CHAPTER 4

Bathrooms

*"I grew up with six brothers. That's how I learned to dance—
waiting for the bathroom."*
—Bob Hope

A bathroom is such small space. Yet no room is more important. Its functions are essential for our comfort and good hygiene. We could live without our guest bedroom more easily than we could live without a bathroom.

However, I'll bet clearing clutter and creating good feng shui in your bathroom is not at the top of your list. Why is that? Is it because you don't spend much time there? Or, is it because it's not one of the gathering places in your home, therefore its condition has less effect on interpersonal interactions? Perhaps the thought of clearing clutter from a bathroom is overwhelming given that it is home to so many different types of small things.

It's funny. Bathrooms, second only to kitchens, are one of the most frequently renovated rooms in a house. Their condition is a factor that can make or break the sale of a house. Yet, when we live in our houses, so often their drawers, vanity cabinets and closets are a jumble of assorted supplies, linens, and toiletries.

You start and end your days in the bathroom. It's decor, organization and energy affect your energy. An attractive, clutter-free and organized bathroom can set the tone for your day and your rest at night.

Bathroom Feng Shui: An Energy and Organizing Challenge

Bathrooms are built with feng shui challenges. Here are a few to consider:

- We urinate and defecate there
- We wash off oils, dirt and grime there
- We flush water down the drain there
- We store an enormous variety of products, tools, and linens there

As you can see, the above functions of the bathroom, though necessary, have negative associations. Yes, we feel better once we are clean and groomed or have relieved ourselves, but the negative associations far outweigh the positive associations.

Feng shui teaches that in order to have good feng shui and feel comfortable in a space there must be a balance of the 5 elements: water, wood, fire, metal, earth. Bathrooms have an abundance of water: in the toilet, the shower, and the sink. Mirrors are also water elements. Plus, many bathrooms still have white walls and tiles (metal elements) which amplify the water element. That's a lot of water! Therefore, the 5 elements

Bathrooms

are significantly out of balance, making it a challenge to make bathrooms feel good.

Plus, water is a symbol for money in feng shui. In bathrooms water is flushed and pours down drains. In other words, money is going down the drain—another feng shui challenge.

Bathrooms also house many different kinds of products and tools ranging from the size of ear plugs to linens. If those things are not kept well organized, they too can be a source of negative energy.

What can be done about the bathroom's feng shui challenges?
- **Keep the toilet seat down** to block the repository of bodily wastes from view and prevent the toilet from sucking positive energies from the room.
- **Keep the bathroom door closed.** I find this hard to do because I enjoy the light coming through my bathroom window which is good energy.
- **Bring color into your bathroom** with your wall color, linens, rugs, bath mats, and art.
- **Paint the walls of the room a color other than white,** cream or a pastel shade, preferably an earth tone (yellow, terra cotta, brown, taupe, sand, etc.). Earth elements dam water and can help balance the water element.
- **Use colorful art, linens, rugs, and bath mats** in shades of blue, purple, green, red, yellow or earth tones to bring in the elements of wood, fire and earth to offset the abundance of water in the room.
- **Clear out items you no longer use and organize the products, tools and linens that you do use.**
- **Keep drawers, vanity cabinets, and the closet organized.**

Because bathrooms start off with so many feng shui challenges, it is important that you give your bathroom as much careful attention as any other room of the house. Make it a place of utter comfort using color and rigorous organization.

Make Your Bathroom Counter Clutter Vanish!

Take a look in your bathroom. What greets you? If your bathroom counter is covered with assorted items like toothpaste, your tooth brush, makeup, lotions, dental floss, jewelry, and other assorted items, notice the thoughts and feelings that come up as you take in the chaos. Perhaps you groan in disgust. Or, think, "What a mess? Do I really need all this stuff?" Or, even worse, "What's wrong with me that I create messes like this?"

If you have negative thoughts and feelings, they occur because every item on the counter is alive with energy. Each one has a different kind of energy. And, the energy of each item is talking to you all at once. That's a lot of noise! Individually each of the items may have a positive energy because it is useful, however, collectively they have a negative energy because there are so many of them in no particular arrangement. The quantity and disorganization of those things create the roar of a crowd.

You might explain the existence of your countertop clutter by saying, "But, I use all those things every morning. It's so convenient to have everything out there." Yes, that may be true, but what if you could still have visibility and convenience as well as a lovely greeting each time you enter your bathroom?

Bathrooms

There are two ways to silence all that noise without sacrificing convenience:

1. **Store those items in drawers and in a cabinet under the sink if you have a vanity that has those types of storage spaces.** The space under sinks in many bathrooms can be as chaotic as the countertops. One option to improve the condition of both the countertop and the vanity cabinet, is to put all the large items you use every day, like deodorant, body lotions, mousse, etc., in one basket or bin under the sink. When you need to use those things, you can grab the basket, place it on the counter, and return it when you are finished using its items. Or, you can leave the bin under the sink and retrieve items from the it, use them, and immediately return them to the bin. Smaller items like makeup, toothbrush, toothpaste, dental floss, lip gloss, etc. can be stored in an easy-to-access drawer, preferably in one of the top two drawers. To prevent drawers from becoming a jumble of miscellaneous things, add several small containers to hold specific items. For example, I have separate containers for makeup, dental floss, and lip glosses in my bathroom drawer?"
2. **Store items in colorful containers placed on the countertop, the back of the toilet, on shelving over the toilet or on shelves in an easy-to-access bathroom closet.** You can have a "used every day" container and separate containers for extra supplies or have separate bins for each category of toiletry you use. To find things easily, I recommend that you assign one category per container. For example, one container could be for all makeup. Another for oral hygiene products. A third for medications used frequently.

Clearing bathroom countertop clutter will accomplish several things:
- **It will immediately transform** your noisy, unattractive, overwhelming and even stressful bathroom into a comfortable place for daily self-care.
- **It will allow you to more easily inventory what you use every day.** With that information you can order products in a timely manner and avoid panic purchases when you run out of products. Because you know exactly what you have, you can prevent purchasing products you already have.
- **It will create the opportunity to discard items** that you no longer use such as empty containers, used tissues, Q-tips, outdated supplies and other accumulated trash.
- **It will be easier to keep your countertop clean.**
- If you create a "use every day" container, what you need will be at your fingertips, and **you will be able to complete your grooming more quickly.**

Bathroom counter clutter creates a feeling of chaos in a place where you start and end your day. The negative energy it generates affects your energy and causes stress. There is much chaos in daily life over which you have no control. Seize control and reduce your stress where you can, starting with your bathroom countertop.

Bathroom Drawers: Mini-Organizing Nightmares

When I pull out bathroom drawers when working with clients in their bathrooms, I hold my breath. What will I find? A neatly organized space or a small dump of miscellaneous items ranging from Q-Tips to

Bathrooms

toothpaste, jewelry and medications. Most often I am greeted with a mishmash of small stuff and feel the urge to shut the drawer and move on to spaces that are more easily organized.

Why do bathroom drawers become small messes?
- **They house many kinds of small items**: makeup, oral hygiene products, medications, eye care items, nail products, lotions, deodorant, hair care items, etc.
- **They are not often thoughtfully set up** with distinct places to put specific items.
- **Things are frequently thrown back into the drawers** after use rather than carefully put away to maintain order in the space.
- **The negative energy of the disorder** that greets you when you open the drawer is off-putting and overwhelming, therefore you are not inclined to restore order to the space.

Spaces with lots of small items can be more daunting to clear than spaces with large items. Add to that the fact that a jumble of toiletries can contain leaking lotions, dust, makeup and hair mixed together. Is it any wonder that clearing out bathroom drawers is often avoided?

What can you do to set up and maintain organized and functional bathroom drawers?
- **Assign each drawer distinct functions.** For example, the top drawer might house items that you use every day. Or, you might assign it the function of holding oral hygiene products (toothpaste, dental floss, etc.) and makeup. Just those two categories of products. The second drawer, if you

have one, could have the function of holding hair products (brushes, combs, hair clips, blow dryer, curling iron). Only hair products. A third drawer could hold occasional use items like nail products, ear plugs, etc. Or, perhaps one of the drawers could hold small first aid items and over-the-counter medications. The key is to limit the number of categories assigned to each drawer and diligently return items to the drawer that houses that type of item.

- **Add small open containers** to separate individual categories of items within each drawer. Assign one category of toiletry per container. For example, as mentioned above, I have three containers in my top bathroom drawer. One holds makeup I use every day. Another holds lip glosses. A third contains dental floss. Your goal is to create distinct locations for each type of toiletry you use. The containers keep like items together and visible. They prevent items of one category from drifting and getting mixed up with items of other categories. In other words, the containers if used for just one type of toiletry can prevent the drawer from melting down into a disorganized mishmash of stuff. Some drawers may not need containers to create structure and maintain order in them. For example, the drawer that houses large hair products like blow dryers, curling irons, and hair brushes may not need any containers. If you add smaller hair products like hair clips and hair ties to the drawer, however, it's best to add a container to hold all those small items together.

- **Return products to their assigned drawer and container after every use.** Resist the urge to throw things back into your drawers without thought when you are in a hurry, perhaps thinking you'll straighten things out later. Later never seems to come. All it takes to plant the seed of a mini-organizing nightmare is to have one or two things out of place in a drawer. Like attracts like. If things are out of place, they will attract more of the same. The order you so carefully set up will melt down very quickly.

Drawers are high use storage areas, often accessed on a daily basis. When they are carefully organized and free of unnecessary items, you'll save time every day because what you need will be at your fingertips, and it will be much easier to get ready for your day.

Is Your Bathroom Vanity Cabinet a Toiletry Dump?

Like vanity drawers, the cabinets in bathroom vanities can easily become cluttered and disorganized spaces. While the drawers are challenging to organize and keep organized because they are small spaces that hold many different types of things, the vanity cabinet can be difficult of keep organized because it is a large open space. It is what I call a black hole. Things go in there and disappear. Because most vanity cabinets typically lack dividers, shelves and compartments, and they are home to many different types of products, they can look and feel like a toiletry dump.

Some folks love trying out new lotions, shampoos, makeup, nail colors and appliances. Unfortunately, when they discover that they don't like a product, instead of giving it away or throwing it away, they shove it into the vanity cabinet. Perhaps they do this because they spent money on it and hate the thought of getting rid of something new. Or, they think they will give it a try at a later date. Or, perhaps someone else will use it. Thus, a dump of castoff stuff is created. Unlike vanity drawers, the cabinets are more difficult to access and therefore typically are used as storage spaces. As such they are more easily neglected. So too are the items stored there.

Plus, another challenge of vanity cabinets is that they are deep spaces. Things stored at the back get lost from view, and therefore are not used. When things aren't regularly accessed, their energy becomes static and negative. Therefore, the back of a vanity cabinet can feel like a graveyard of dead toiletries, tools and supplies.

To transform your under-the-counter bathroom dump into a more active, useful storage area, first clear the space of items you dislike, never use, find annoying to use or that are broken, out of date or just plain nasty. Be sure to have several garbage bags on hand. You will be amazed at the quantity of things that you toss out.

Now you are ready to create a new order in your vanity. Following are suggestions for making it a more functional space:

- **Only store small products in this area that are in containers of like items.** Small things get lost in that big space among big supplies.
- **Add a wire cabinet shelf organizer to create two levels within the cabinet.** That will break up the large, open space and create a more structured space.
- **Store only large, tall and easily visible items at the back of the cabinet.** For example, stacks of toilet paper are easily seen. Or, you could position large boxes of appliances or stacks of towels in that area.
- **Use bins to store categories of supplies.** The bins create

structure and obvious homes for each category of item stored under the sink. For example, you could have separate bins for extra hair products, soaps, extra makeup, lotions, cleaning products, etc.

- **Place bins of the items you use most often at the front of the cabinet.**
- **Give yourself a reason to access the vanity cabinet on a regular basis.** To make it easy to do my morning grooming I set up a bin for all the larger toiletries that I use daily. Rather than leave them on the vanity countertop, I store them below and pull out and put back what I need each day. That bin contains a mix of medium-size items: hair spray, mouthwash, body lotion, deodorant, air freshener, mousse for hair styling. Everything I need is at my fingertips.

Reclaim your vanity cabinets by clearing out old, grimy, unused or rarely used toiletries, supplies, appliances and linens. Then create a new structure in them that allows you to see everything stored there in one glance and easily restore order when necessary.

The Bathroom Closet: Challenges and Solutions

If you have a bathroom closet, count yourself lucky. Not all bathrooms have that wonderful, large storage area. Like vanity drawers and the vanity cabinet, keeping bathroom closets clear of clutter and organized can be a challenge.

Here's why:
- **Bathroom closets have doors** and their contents are out of sight, therefore, out of mind
- **Bathroom closets often house items as diverse** as linens and first aid supplies
- **Closet shelves are often deep**, which creates visibility problems
- **Upper shelves, lower shelves, and the floor area** are difficult to see and access
- **The size of items in the closet can range** from very small (nail polish bottles) to very large (blankets, sheets, towels)

It isn't necessary to completely empty the bathroom closet to clear it of clutter and reorganize it. In fact, emptying the closet is likely to be overwhelming. Some sorting and purging of things can be done within the closet if space allows. Working on one shelf at a time can prevent overwhelm.

In other chapters I recommend clearing all clutter first before reorganizing spaces. In the bathroom, however, it isn't necessary to purge the whole closet at once. You can clear clutter one shelf at a time. Or, clear items that are worn out, never used, or infrequently used as you are working on a particular category of items. For example, you've decided to relocate your linens. As you move them, note their condition and how often you use them. Keep only those things that are in good condition and used at some point during the span of a year.

The small items in a bathroom closet can easily become a cluttered mess, and form an overwhelming, negative energy that can shut down even the most competent brain. Therefore, it's best to first address the big stuff in a bathroom closet, the linens. Linens can be stored on those

Bathrooms

hard-to-see upper or lower shelves because they are large and easy to see. If you have enough shelf space, it is best to separate sheets and other bedding from towels, and place them on different shelves. Use the top shelf for big occasional use items like extra bathroom rugs, pillows, and blankets.

Once you have put linens in place, move on to creating homes for other large items like jugs of shampoo, heating pads and other large first aid supplies such as ankle, wrist, and knee supports and splints, and toiletry bags. As you sort, ask yourself, "Do I use this? How likely is it that I will use it? When was the last time I used it?" Let go of anything you don't use or haven't used in a very long time. The large items that remain can also be placed on upper or lower shelves because their size makes them more easily visible. Be sure to place similar items together. For example, all travel items together, all toiletry products together, etc.

When all the large items have homes, it will be much easier to address all the little stuff.

Clump like items together, all nail products together, all oral hygiene projects together, all over-the-counter medications together, all first aid supplies together, etc. As you separate things into categories, look for things that are very old, outdated, never used or seldom used, or just plain yucky that can be tossed in the trash.

When you have finished sorting and purging small things, create a home for each category of item. In order to easily access small items, they must be easy to reach and visible. Therefore, they are best located on shelves that are located between abdomen and eye level. I call those shelves "prime real estate." Small things should NEVER be placed on upper and lower shelves unless you have a substantial quantity which makes them visible.

If small children have access to your bathroom closet, be sure to locate medications and other toxic substances out of reach or restrict access to the closet. Do the same in all other areas that house toxic and dangerous supplies such as under the kitchen sink, in the utility room, and in the garage.

Use a plastic bin or a small plastic drawer to hold each category of small item. Place infrequently used items behind those bins, striving to make each one visible.

Once you have created a new order in your bathroom closet, your next challenge is to make yourself regularly return items to their new homes after use. That's pretty easy to do with linens. To maintain an organized, highly functional bathroom closet, also be sure to take the extra few seconds to place smaller items in their appropriate containers.

Bathrooms

Bathroom Clutter Clearing Plan

The articles above give a lot of information about how to clear clutter and organize the bathroom countertop, bathroom drawers, vanity cabinets and the bathroom closet. Therefore, this plan will outline general guidelines that apply to all areas of the bathroom.

1. **Take "before" photos of each bathroom as a whole, each countertop, drawer, vanity cabinet and closet if you have one.** As you look at those photos, notice how you feel. Do you feel overwhelmed by the noise of the clutter? Or, are you excited to get started? If you feel overwhelmed, take a deep breath and tell yourself that you can get started if you start by looking for large things that can be thrown away.

2. **Begin clutter clearing with the countertop only if it visually disturbs and distracts you from making progress in other areas.** I generally don't recommend starting with the countertop because the goal for clearing a countertop is to store items found there either in drawers or in the vanity cabinet. You must first clear out those areas to have space for the items on the countertop.

3. **Start clearing in the vanity cabinet or in the bathroom closet** because those two areas typically house larger items and are likely to be less overwhelming to approach than the drawers or countertop. When large items are cleared first, you will immediately see and feel progress, feelings of overwhelm will diminish, and you'll be motivated to keep clearing.

4. **Once the vanity cabinet and closet are done, clear the**

drawers and the countertop. That clearing will be easier to do because large areas have already been cleared.

5. **Start each area looking for things that are easy to get rid of.** When you do an immediate purge, energies in the space will shift from negative to positive, making it easier to keep going. Look for outdated grooming products; prescriptions or over-the-counter medications that are past their expiration dates; worn out appliances and linens; broken things, and things that you never use, rarely use, or are unlikely to use in the future.

6. **Separate items you use every day from items that are used or accessed only occasionally.** Locate everyday items in easy-to-access areas like the drawers and/or in bins at the front of the vanity cabinet. Store extra supplies and occasional use items either in the back of the vanity cabinet or in the closet.

7. **In each area, clump like items together in categories.** For example, put bed linens with bed linens, towels with towels, hair products with hair products, extra supplies with extra supplies, medications with medications, etc.

8. **Never store small items on upper shelves or at the back of shelves.** They won't be visible, and therefore won't be used.

9. **Store containers of small things in areas that are most visible and most easy to access.** That would be in drawers, at the front of the vanity cabinets, and on shelves between abdomen and eye level.

10. **Put each category of small items into a single open bin, basket, or a plastic drawer.** Avoid putting several categories in one container because it will be more difficult to organize,

Bathrooms

keep organized, and find what you need when you need it.

11. **Store large items on upper and lower shelves in the closet, on the closet floor or at the back of the vanity cabinet.**
12. **Take "after" photos of the whole bathroom, the drawers, countertop, vanity cabinet, and the closet.** Compare those photos to the "before" photos. Now, how do you feel now?

From Cluttered to Clear in Just One Year

CHAPTER 5

Home Office

"You can tell if a person is organized by checking his desktop."
—Ali AlJa'bari

The home office. Not all people designate one room as a home office. If you have one, I'm sure you know its biggest challenge: PAPER! The home office is another room in the house, like the bedroom, that is often neglected. I wonder if it gets neglected because its primary functions rarely rank up there as favorites for most people: bill-paying and filing. Or, perhaps its association with paper keeps homeowners from investing much time in creating fully functional, organized and clutter-free home offices. After all, many people procrastinate dealing with paper at least some of the time.

Regardless of how you feel about your home office, it is a space where survival activities occur. By survival, I mean activities that are essential to your well-being. The quality of your financial well-being has a profound effect on your quality of life. The condition of your home office affects the quality of your financial well-being and your peace of mind. A clutter-free and organized home office sets the stage for good financial management. Whereas, a home office that has never been fully organized and has become a drop spot for papers and a whole host of other things makes every aspect of financial management more difficult.

How Does Your Home Office Make You Feel?

The first step before making any improvements to your home office is to think about how it makes you feel . . .

When you look at your home office, do you cringe? Many people do. Why is that? I think there are three primary reasons that home offices become places to avoid: 1) they often hold functions that most people want to avoid; bill-paying, financial management, and paper storage, 2) they are often unattractively appointed, and 3) they are cluttered with paper.

No matter how much money you make, you probably still feel some discomfort when it comes to paying bills and managing your finances. Were you ever taught how to handle paper? Not likely! So, quite possibly it's an area not only associated with money anxiety, but also paper incompetence. Doesn't that make you so excited about spending time there, doing boring tasks like paying bills and filing? Heck, no!

Unless you use your home office for a home-based business that generates enough income to pay for high quality office furniture, most home offices are furnished with furniture leftovers doubling as office furniture; folding tables and cheap office furniture from office supply chain stores. You end of up with a hodge-podge of furnishings that are difficult to make look attractive. As for wall color, if funds are tight, you'll paint other rooms attractive colors yet hold off on painting the home office a pleasant color. Attractive art in the home office? Why bother! After all, nobody sees it but family members, who don't even spend much time there!

Add to that the fact that home offices often are multi-purpose rooms that are also used as guest and craft rooms. When rooms have more than one purpose, it's easy for their essential functions to become blurred. They eventually end up as dumping grounds for things you don't know what to do with, things you don't want to take the time to move up to the attic, and things you need to clear from other rooms when company is coming.

If by now you're feeling sorry for your home office, good! It's the brain of the house, the home of crucial functions like financial management, and is worthy of more respect. If I told you the condition of your home office could be affecting both your current finances and your financial future, would you treat it with more respect? If I told you that disorder in that room creates a mental fogginess that could affect all decision-making, would that motivate you to create a new order there? Would you be more willing to spend some time and money to make it an attractive place so you will be more comfortable doing essential tasks like bill-paying? I hope so.

If you decide to make your home office a personal paradise, a place where you would enjoy spending time, what would it look like? Because the functions of a home office cause discomfort and anxiety, it is essential that you create a lovely, comfortable space that will seduce you to cross the threshold to do the dreaded tasks of filing and bill-paying. Have fun with it! The time and expense are well worth it!

Your Home Office Is the Brain of Your Home

Home offices are rarely treated with the respect they deserve. They often become dumping grounds for everything paper and more. When you consider that, at the very least, your home office is often the administrative and *financial center of the home*, you would think that they'd all be in tip top shape. But, they're not. In fact, most of those I've seen are not. Why is that?

Here are some possibilities:
- **That room may accurately reflect your relationship with your financial situation**
- **It could reflect that the room was never set up for optimal functioning**, either because you did not make time for the set up or because you really didn't know how to set it up
- **The home office may accurately reflect your aptitude for organizing paper,**
- **The home office may be a reflection of your inability to be disciplined** about doing tasks that are detailed, boring and time-consuming
- **You may not have a grasp on the connection** between the condition of your home office and your financial well-being and peace of mind
- **You have a very full plate**, and "tending" to the home office requires more mental energy than you can muster on a regular basis
- **Maintaining an orderly, clutter-free home office** simply is not a priority

Home Office

Home offices also often have the unfortunate fate of being multipurpose rooms. They are frequently the leftover bedroom used for housing many functions like bill-paying, records storage, gift-wrapping center, sewing room, guest room and play room. As a multipurpose room, its significance as a hub for financial and administrative management for the household is often diminished. Setting up and maintaining order in a multipurpose room is much more challenging than having a room devoted to household paperwork and finances.

Where to begin? The fate of the home office starts with understanding its importance relative to other rooms in the house. If you run a business from a home office, its significance is apparent. But, if your home office is just "paper central" (a place to store papers and pay bills), plus a few other functions like the gift-wrapping center and guest room, it's harder to get clear about its purpose.

Perhaps this reminder will help: the home office is the brain of your home. Let me repeat that again: your home office is the brain of your home. This is the place where essential information is stored relating to finances and running your household (and your life!). Like your brain, when it is up to par, you can handle whatever life throws at you. If your brain is foggy and unfocused, it's difficult to make decisions and navigate through life. So too with the home office. A cluttered, messy home office not only radiates negative energy but presents problems when you need to lay your hands on an important record or pay a bill in a timely fashion.

So, your first step in creating a home office that you enjoy is to shift your mindset. Start thinking about your home office as the brain of your home... focused, clear, and open to receiving new opportunities (including financial growth!).

From Cluttered to Clear in Just One Year

Three Important Steps to Unpacking Boxes in Your Home Office

Setting up a home office can feel overwhelming. What is the best location for all the different types of items that make up your office? Just the quantity of all the items that need to be organized alone can shut you down. When I helped one of my long-term clients set up her home office, she kept taking deep breaths and saying, "Oh, my!" every time I brought in a new box and unpacked it. She wasn't alone! I, too, experienced the gut-clenching feeling of, "Oh my! What do I do with all this stuff?" It is normal to feel that way. Don't let the feeling of overwhelm stop you from setting up your home office!

When unpacking to set up your office, good is good enough. Experience has taught me to push past the uncomfortable feelings that come up when setting up a space. Notice the feeling and then just make the best guess for the optimal placement of everything. I've learned that aiming for perfection when initially setting up a space will keep you from unpacking anything or will set you up to feel like a failure when you don't make the best decisions about placement.

Initially it's most important to get everything out of the boxes and the boxes removed. Then, follow these three steps:

1. **Clump items by category.** For example, all the office supplies will go together. Within the supplies category, clump together like items: paper, software, writing implements, file folders, envelopes, and small supplies like staples, push pins, tape, post-it notes, etc.
2. **Place those clumped categories based on how often you**

access each of them. The ones you and your family often grab ideally should be located within easy reach of the desk.
3. **Once things are initially put away, use the space for a while.** Taking time to do this step will help you fine-tune its organization. If something isn't in the best location, you'll feel irritated by the effort it takes to retrieve or put it away. Or, it will bug you to have something you seldom use in your face all the time, taking up prime real estate. That irritation is your cue to make an adjustment in location. Move the things that you use the most to positions closer to you, and move things you seldom or only occasionally use further away from you.

The next time you have to unpack a home office, cut yourself some slack! Don't expect to organize it perfectly the first time. Organizing is a process, a process of figuring out what works best over time. Get things unpacked and placed in the most logical locations. Remember, it's likely that you'll have to move things around a bit once you start using the space. That's part of the process, not a sign of incompetence or failure!

Tips for Finding Calm Out of Home Office Chaos

I walked into a home office lined with piles. Everywhere I looked there were piles of papers and other miscellaneous stuff. My first instinct was to turn around and return to my client's living room, where I felt so much more comfortable. That's the truth! Yes, even professional organizers want to run away from piles of stuff and the multitude of decisions to be made if they are ever to be dissolved.

From Cluttered to Clear in Just One Year

Instead of running, however, I got on my knees on the floor and started looking for a place to begin. You see, there's usually a way into a cluttered mess like that. What am I talking about? It's as if something is holding all that chaos in place that if discovered and dismantled would offset the negative energy of the paper challenge and shift energies from negative to positive, making the clutter seem less daunting.

Finding the Calm Out of Chaos

In this case the key was a box of audiobooks on CD. I found it when I was examining the contents of the piles, looking for big chunks of things that could be easily moved. I asked my client where she kept her audiobooks. She laughed and said, "Oh, everywhere!"

I happened to know that this client is a seeker, someone who loves learning and who really values her audiobooks. And there they were, buried in her neglected piles. I said, "We've got to create one space for all your audiobooks! They are too important to be floating around!" She agreed and allowed me to search out a spot.

Lest you think I never have doubts about whether I'm doing the right thing in the right moment, you need to know that I did find myself wondering if working on the CDs was the right place to begin. I've done this long enough, however, to know that trusting my intuition works better than acting on my doubts. So, I kept going.

Getting the Ball Rolling and Creating a "New Order"

The CDs came to rest in bins on shelves in one corner of her office. The act of organizing and placing her CDs all together in one location had an amazing effect on our ability to make progress in that cluttered room. Not only did it get the ball rolling, but the movement of that one chunk of the mess shifted the energy in that home office from stagnation to movement, from negative to positive. After moving the CDs to a real home, my client and I plowed through the rest of those piles in record time. We literally felt something akin to a high from the positive energy we had generated by creating a new order for items of real significance.

Are you avoiding an organizing challenge in your home office, perhaps one that is complicated by the negative energy of paper? See if you can find the key that will unlock the door to your resistance. By the way, it's not likely to be paper! *Look for something of significance that you can easily move and honor* by giving it a home.

Then, enjoy the ride!

Uncovering Your Emotional Blocks

"He's very nervous about you coming," Gail said as we were working in her house, clearing clutter. She was talking about her boyfriend, who had reluctantly agreed to accept a consultation with me as a gift. I wasn't surprised by her comment. It's very common for people to want help to reclaim peace and comfort in their physical spaces, yet they are terrified about their clutter being seen.

Your house is an extension of yourself. It tells the truth about what's going on in your life. If, for a while, your life is a bit out of control because of stressors (like illness, deaths of friends and family members, divorce, depression, having children, or moving), the condition of your home often reflects the stress.

In this case, I had been warned that the house had gotten pretty backed up with stuff. When I entered the home office, it really looked like a storeroom with boxes piled at least five feet high in the center of the room. I asked my new client, "What's in these boxes?" I was very surprised that he actually remembered what was in those boxes.

"They are things that belonged to my mother and sister."

With a little probing, I learned that those women had died seven and four years previously. The boxes had taken up residence in that room following their deaths.

You may be amazed that nothing had been done with those boxes for so many years. Why wouldn't he have felt compelled to dismantle the box pile that was blocking access to his desk, bookshelf and keyboard? This man was a musician; music was a passion! What would stop him dead in his tracks? **Grief.**

As we worked and talked, I learned that this man's relationship with both his mother and sister had been problematic, painful, and even scary at times. His family was affected by the insanity of alcoholism, a disease that affects every family member in some way. So, what's that got to do with the items in those boxes?

Items owned by a person hold that person's energy. A deceased person may be physically gone, but their belongings hold their energy. It's common to be assaulted by old memories when you encounter things associated with a particular person. Intuitively my client knew that if he opened those boxes, he was going back in time. He was probably not conscious that his avoidance of opening those boxes was fueled by a reluctance to face old memories, old sadness and loss. However, the pain of those memories held in place by the objects had kept him stuck for years.

We made it through the stack of boxes, clearing space in my client's home office and breaking through his emotional barriers as well. I could tell that the feelings of grief had lifted a bit and there was new space, both physically and emotionally, for new, good things to enter.

What objects in your home office space hold sadness in place,

blocking you from moving forward with your life? Check out those areas that you have been neglecting. Is there an emotional block keeping you stuck? Getting conscious of a painful association is the first step. Bring it to consciousness, allow the feelings that come up, so you can let them go, and move on.

Jumpstart Your Life; Clear Your Dead Computers

Would you keep dead bugs in your home office? Certainly not! But, I'll bet at one time or another you've held on to a dead computer. When a computer isn't being used, its energy goes dead and becomes negative, just like the negative energy of dead bugs.

Negative energy affects your energy and can block your access to positive energy, opportunities and prosperity. Can you afford not to move those dead bodies?

Why do computers hang out once they've been replaced by a newer model? A common reason is that they still hold information. Not knowing how to clear that information is a barrier to getting rid of those beasts. Another reason is that people don't know how to get rid of them. Who wants an outdated computer?

Take action with these two steps:
1. **Schedule time this week to clear the information off those dead beasts.** Make it happen! Your dead computers are not serving you and your life. Either clear the computer files yourself, or call your favorite computer guru and schedule a time for him/her to do it for you. Remember that it's not enough to simply delete files; all personal data must be fully

removed. All it takes is a phone call to set an appointment to make it happen.

2. **Take those outdated machines to Goodwill or another charity that recycles them.** those organizations will put them to good use.

Once you've taken those two steps, your home office will feel so much better. You will have more energy available to you, and you will have helped others with their computer needs.

Last but no least: make sure you celebrate the steps you've taken. Kudos!!

Seven Home Office Self-Seduction Tips

Feng shui teaches that your goal when you arrange a space is to create a personal paradise. No room needs that approach more than a home office. As one of the most neglected and most dumped-in rooms in the house, it really needs some thoughtful attention and positive energy to make it an appealing place to work.

But, where to start? How exciting are filing cabinets, bookcases, desks and computer equipment?

> **TIP #1: Start with the wall color.** It will set the tone and serve as the foundation for all other enhancements you make. Painting the walls a color is imperative. White walls very quickly become dingy, scarred and dirty. It is also easy to feel anxious and de-

pressed in rooms with white walls because the colors of prints, photographs and paintings on the walls just won't show up. We physiologically need color in our environment to feel good. It nurtures us with its energy. Paint your home office walls a color. Colors I recommend for home offices are a buttery yellow, sage green, and my new favorite, an earthy turquoise blue. Blues and greens are associated with the wood element. The wood element in feng shui is associated with growth and expansion and a positive, upward energy. Yellow is an optimistic earth element.

TIP #2: Eliminate any furniture that is broken, ugly or doesn't work well. You want all your furnishings to have good energy. It's likely that you'll be using odds and ends in this room, i.e., furniture that isn't needed elsewhere. In addition to being functional, make sure that you actually like each piece and that all the pieces look good together.

TIP #3: Eliminate fluorescent lighting, and be sure to have multiple incandescent light sources. It's a good idea to have some up-lighting as well, light that is directed up toward the ceiling. Light is energy. You'll need plenty of energy to face the types of tasks typically done in a home office.

TIP #4: Place the desk in the power position with a solid wall behind it and a full view of the door. From that position, your nervous system will relax, and you will feel empowered and ready to tackle whatever awaits you on the desk.

TIP #5: Place other furniture around the desk, both to accommodate the convenient completion of the tasks to be done at the desk and to look attractive.

TIP #6: Add plants to bring the outdoors inside. Green is an optimistic color. Live or silk plants can immediately change the feel of a room that has lots of hard edges and electrical equipment. They provide a soft, soothing energy. Make sure that live plants are healthy and have round leaves. Avoid dried plants and those with thorns and pointed shapes. Dried plants have a dead energy, especially when their color fades. Thorns and pointed leaves hold negative energies because of their potential to do physical harm.

TIP #7: Add art, photographs, and special mementoes you love, anything that makes your heart sing and that empowers you. For example, I have a photograph of me that was taken with Jack Canfield at a conference years ago. Jack is one of my mentors. He doesn't know it, but I want to do the kind of work he's been so successful doing. I want to share my message with the world like he has. I also framed a print of the Chinese letters for "feng shui," since feng shui is a focus of all the work I do. When I recently re-decorated my office, I deliberately chose to limit all other art on the walls to original art by artists I know.

Invest in making your home office a personal paradise, and you'll want to spend more time there. You'll also be more motivated to treat it with the respect it deserves! Wouldn't it be nice to *love* your home office? You can! Make it so!

Do the Images in Your Workspace Support Success?

Because your home office is a place where figuratively money is coming in and going out, it tends to be a room that has the potential to hold stressful energy. Like many, you may be thinking, "Why bother putting real art up in this utilitarian place that I'd rather avoid?"

Let me suggest another perspective. There are some very specific images that will *support* your success and create an environment where you'll want to be. Yes, the home office is related to the financial survival of the family and record keeping, but it's also a place where you can do creative thinking and problem-solving, where you can feel a sense of accomplishment.

If the room is clutter-free and organized, all of that will come so much easier. Life will run more smoothly. When problems arise, they can be resolved quickly.

With those more positive images in mind, think about subjects and art that will enhance your space, both to send a positive message about the importance of the functions of the room and to attract you into the room.

From Cluttered to Clear in Just One Year

I suggest the following empowering images:
- **Mountain scenes**
- **Positive ACTION or ACHIEVEMENT** scenes like sailing, mountain climbing, skiing, flying, or any activity you love doing
- **Scenes that evoke a feeling** of action with a "Yes, I can!" attitude
- **High energy images with bold colors**, especially reds, greens and blues

The home office is also a great place to display diplomas and certificates of achievement, anything that is *evidence of your accomplishments and competence.* **Preserve those memories by incorporating diplomas and photos that remind you of happy, successful times.**

For years my undergraduate and graduate diplomas hung in my home office. I also displayed certificates I had received from feng shui trainings and other certificate programs, like Reality Therapy and the Myers Briggs Type Indicator.

I also created and hung a framed piece that held a newspaper article about Simply Organized, my organizing business, a photograph of me presenting a seminar, and my company logo. When I changed my company name to Rock Scissors Paper Institute, I created another framed piece showing images of rocks and other objects from nature and my new logo. Those framed pieces were enhancements that kept me grounded in my competence and helped me focus on my business.

Add in images of positive influence. Also consider displaying photographs of people who had a positive influence in your life. As I mentioned previously, front and center in my office is a photograph of Jack Canfield and me that was taken at a conference of the National Association of Professional Organizers. Jack doesn't know me personally, nor I him. But, I admire the contribution he has made to our world with his *Chicken Soup for the Soul* books, his teachings, and the behavior he models for other evolving souls and entrepreneurs. I want to make a big difference for good, as he has done. I also want what I teach to travel the world, as his teachings have. That photograph reminds me of what I want and what is possible.

Don't forget images of beauty to create positive energy that makes you feel good. Use the art in your home office as a way to empower yourself to stay on track and do those difficult tasks you'd rather avoid. Thoughtfully and intentionally adding art to your home office is an opportunity to use the positive energy of art for your own good. What is good for you is good for your family and our world.

Tackling Dead Bodies (Difficult Tasks) in Your Home Office

I'll bet when you think of your home office files you groan. I do! I'd been meaning to do some clearing in my home office files for several months before I finally got started. Why is it so easy to ignore home office files, especially when we know we'll feel so good when we get rid of all those useless papers?

Did you know that 80 to 90 percent of paper in files *never* gets touched again? We avoid doing it because it's a boring task that could make you want to throw up! I'm not kidding about that! One of my clients threw up during a paper clutter clearing session! When I think about slogging my way through old, dead papers, my gut hurts! Does yours?

From Cluttered to Clear in Just One Year

So, what exactly is it about clearing files that makes us want to throw up? As you know, feng shui teaches that everything is alive with energy. Everything vibrates with some type of energy. The energy of stagnant files, those that have been sitting for years without being accessed, tends to diminish with time. Stagnation of anything leads to death. Papers that don't move and that are of no use have a dead energy. Keeping old, useless papers around is like keeping dead bodies in your home office. You wouldn't keep dead animals in your home office, so why would you keep dead papers?

I finally made progress clearing out my files after several years of avoidance. The last time I went through them was so boring that the memory of that time kept me from facing the challenge. But, once I cleared every other area of my office except my files it was time to find a way to take action. Believe it or not, I could feel the dead energy of those files every time I entered my home office. Also, according to feng shui, they were located in the health and creativity/children areas of my home office! *That stagnant, dead energy could have attracted health issues and could have affected my creative efforts in my business and my life!*

How did I get started? *I made a public commitment to clear out my file cabinets.* Years ago, I wrote in my blog about how to transform your life with clutter clearing. Because I thought I should practice what I was preaching I wrote openly about my commitment to clear out my files in my newsletter and on my business Facebook page.

I also wanted to take my message "Clear Clutter for Good!®" worldwide. Because of that important goal, I could not afford to have two major energy blocks in my office: two packed filing cabinets.

I took one step at a time to feel the progress. Instead of attempting to clear a whole cabinet in one day, as I had done before, I decided to do five files per day, for as long as it took to get the job done. Five files were enough to feel like I was making progress, yet not so much that it seemed overwhelming.

I had to address several challenges, like how to remember to go through files every day and how to get back to it after being out of town for several days. What finally worked for me was to keep a small post-it note on my kitchen counter that said, "Clear Five Files." Because I had no other post-it notes on the counter, and because it was bright green, I saw it many times per day. It bugged me. It was my cue to pull five files from the cabinet and go through them. At first, I tried to do the clearing at my desk, because the cabinets were next to it. But, I found myself feeling reluctant to spend even more time away from Bob, my husband, than I was already doing. I ended up pulling the five files each night and going through them when we are watching TV. Multi-tasking is generally not recommended, because it negatively affects productivity and accuracy, however, neither issue was of great importance when eliminating dead bodies from my files and watching TV.

Celebrate the completion of each step. I am happy to report that I finished going through all four drawers. The reward for any celebrated completion is a nice serotonin burst in the brain. In other words, you get rewarded when you complete tasks and celebrate them. If you forego the celebration, you won't receive the serotonin reward. So, celebrate all completions, especially when you clear out files!

When will you tackle the dead bodies in your home office? Don't start until you've cleared everything else in your space except paper. That way, the positive energy you've created by the clearing larger items will support your efforts, and you'll find it easier to think clearly. Remove those dead bodies and watch the energy in your home office improve!

Establish Home Office Boundaries and Expectations

I'll admit right up front that I'm writing this section especially for those of you who complain about children invading your home office.

You may not have a clue how to stop the offending behavior, or perhaps you don't want to make waves. One thing is for sure, with the advent of the computer, the home office has become a more attractive place for children of all ages. After all, you can play games on the computer. You can email friends. You can enjoy social media. You can look up fascinating information.

Unfortunately, what so often doesn't happen is parents setting specific boundaries and expectations for acceptable behavior in the space. All too often what happens is that children quite naturally take up residence in the space and leave it trashed when they depart. It's not surprising, therefore, that many of you end up feeling annoyed and throw up your hands about this dilemma. What's needed is for you to make time to explain to children that use of the home office and its equipment is a privilege contingent on their behavior and their ability to treat the space with the respect it deserves.

Is Maintaining an Orderly Office Even Possible?

Yes, however, being able to maintain an uncluttered home office is only possible if every person who uses the space does their part to maintain order. In other words, everyone must know the expectations. They must be committed to picking up after themselves, throwing trash away, and removing dirty dishes and glasses. Remember, the home office is the brain of your home. It's energy profoundly affects mental clarity, par-

Home Office

ticularly in the area of home finances.

Because children by nature tend to primarily be self-serving, and may not be aware of how their behavior affects others, you might find it's easier to make arrangements for them to use a computer in some location other than the home office. If they're permitted to use the space, make sure they know your expectations and consequences for not meeting those expectations. Then, if they fail to pick up after themselves, you are prepared to follow through with the consequences. You will not only be teaching them a valuable lesson, you will also be assuring that your home office is maintained as a comfortable and fully functional room in your home . . . for your entire family.

Home Office Clutter Clearing Plan

Clutter in a home office is equivalent to blockages in the circuitry of your brain. As you know, blockages in the brain can be lethal. They can also cause a state of unease that results in stress, anxiety and fear, and impairs productivity. When your home office is clear of clutter you can access the information you need for personal business and personal interests within seconds. Once you have ready access to that information, your life can roll along more smoothly.

Clearing clutter from the home office can feel like you've gotten your brain back! Let me show you how.

1. **Take a photo of your home office before you begin work.** As you look at it, take note of the "hot" spots, those areas of intense negative energy that make you want to run from the room. Resist the urge to run. Notice the negative thoughts that immediately pop up. Thoughts like, "What a mess! I don't know where to start. This will take forever to do!" Negative thoughts when facing a congested and cluttered home office are normal, however, they aren't necessarily telling the truth. Pay attention to those thoughts, but don't allow them to shut down your brain. Tell yourself, "This is not helpful. This clearing can be done one step at a time. I can get help to do it if I need it." Focus on the challenge areas. The truth is that clearing out the home office may take time, especially because it is a paper haven, but you can do it. You may have to do it in a number of short sessions or get some help to make it so.

2. **If paper has gone wild in the room, gather it up and**

put it in bags or boxes to deal with after you've finished organizing the rest of the room. As you gather up the papers, be sure to separate out supplies like envelopes, writing implements, sheet protectors and pads of paper. Put those aside in one area of the room. Also, be sure not to scoop up papers associated with current bills to be paid and current action items. Keep those two categories of paper separate from the rest of the paper. That way you can keep up with bills and other important actions that must be handled before the clutter clearing and organizing is completed. The purpose of gathering up the paper is to quiet its annoying, distressing and distracting negative energy so you can think clearly as you make decisions about the rest of the contents of the room.

3. **If there are miscellaneous little items floating around the room, on the desk, filing cabinet, floor, etc., gather them all up and put them in a bag or basket.** Like paper, the energy of those little things can be very distracting and needs to be silenced before moving forward. You can deal with those things at the end of the clutter clearing process, once everything bigger has been handled.

4. **Identify all the functions of the room.** Home offices are often multi-purpose rooms, especially in small houses. It's important to determine the various functions of the room before you begin clutter clearing, so you'll know what things belong in the room and what needs to find a home elsewhere. Is it just a home office, a place to pay bills and store papers you might need to access someday? Does it house a home-based business as well as personal financial

information? Is the room both home office and guest room? Does it also serve as the location of the gift-wrapping center for the home? Is it a craft room as well as a home office? So many possibilities! Know that the more functions housed in a room, the more challenging it will be to organize and keep organized.

5. **Remove everything from the space that does not fit its functions.** Place those things either just inside or just outside the door to be moved once you've worked long enough to have either a weary brain, or to have accumulated enough items to justify taking a break to distribute them to their new locations.

6. **Look at each piece of furniture and determine whether it serves at least one of the functions of the room.** Remove any furniture that doesn't serve one of the functions you've identified. Because home offices are complicated spaces that are a challenge to organize and keep organized, and ALWAYS have a lot going on in them, you cannot afford to have excess furniture holding precious energy that could be better used in another way in that room.

7. **Check each piece of furniture to make sure it works well and is in good condition.** A good way to determine this is by noticing which furniture is being used and which is not. If something is not being used, why not? It's common that filing cabinets and desks with broken drawers or drawers that don't open and close easily will be avoided. Let go of furnishings that are not in good condition.

8. **Check the placement of the furniture.** Is it comfortable? Is the desk situated so you will be in the power position,

having a full view of the door and a solid wall behind you? Is it possible to work effectively and efficiently in the current arrangement? If you feel irritated and/or unsettled when working at the desk, or if you avoid the space altogether, rearrange the furniture being sure that you put yourself in the power position when working at the desk. Make sure you can easily reach anything you will use on a regular basis, like computers, printers, other office equipment, filing cabinets, and supplies.

9. **When you are moving furniture around, be sure to clump supplies you encounter in one location** for evaluation, organizing and containing later in the clutter clearing process.

10. **Evaluate computer equipment.** Does it all work? If there are old computers, printers, modems and hard drives that are not being used, why not? Purge broken items that aren't worth repairing, items you don't know how to use and don't care about figuring out how to use. The "someday" you think will come to figure out everything is not likely to arrive. Get real about all the electronic equipment that you own. Make decisions about what will be kept and let go of the rest. As mentioned previously, this may require taking steps to remove data from hard drives. Remember, if you are not computer savvy, the fastest way to clear hard drives is to hire someone to do it for you. There are companies that will buy used electronic equipment, however, it is work to research such companies, comply with their requirements, and pack up and mail your equipment. Experience has taught me that many people have good intentions to follow through with

that process, but avoid it like the plague. It is a complicated, boring task. In fact, clients sometimes pay me to complete that task because they can't make themselves do it. An easier option is to donate electronics to charities, like Goodwill, that will recycle them. Live only with electronic equipment that is alive and used!

11. **Gather all books together and evaluate the energy of each one.** Books to keep are those that are still alive with positive energy. That includes books you haven't read, but are still interested in reading; those that you have read and are likely to re-read; those that you will reference, and any book that has changed your life. Let go of the rest.

12. **If you have binders, evaluate each one to determine if it is worth keeping.** Binders from workshops and conferences are seldom used after the event and can take up valuable "real estate" in a home office. If you don't use a binder in the first month after a workshop or conference, you are unlikely to ever use it. Let it go! Binders of old financial information can be archived in banker's boxes in the attic, again freeing up precious space in the home office. If, like me, you've had good intentions to use binders, but really hate or avoid the hole punching process, consider getting rid of binders in favor of another way of storing important papers.

13. **Sort supplies by category:** writing implements, paper, filing supplies, index cards, sheet protectors, binders, blank CDs, jewel cases, organizing supplies, etc. As you sort, put aside any supplies you no longer use, that are outdated, and that you find annoying or irritating to use. They can be donated or thrown away. Once the supplies are sorted by type, look

at the quantity of each item. If you have an excessive amount of any item, consider donating a portion of it to a local charity. After you've made those decisions, check to see if all the supplies you plan to keep will fit in the storage area you plan to use to house them. Make it your goal to have all your supplies comfortably live in the storage space available.

14. **Evaluate all software books and CDs** (manuals, music, software, photos, audiobooks, etc.)**,** purging any that are outdated or that you no longer use.

15. **Consider all the decorative items in the space.** Do they still have positive energy? Do you love or use them? If not, let them go. Or, if you have a decorative item that you still love, but no longer want in the home office, put it by the door to find a home for it in another part of the house.

16. **Check out any other items** that don't fit into the major categories I've discussed to whether you still love or use them. Move things that don't meet that criteria to the door and place them with other items to be donated.

17. **Once the entire space has been evaluated and unused and unloved items purged, turn your attention toward the paper that you scooped up early in the clutter clearing process.** This might be easier to do if you remove trash, items to be donated and items that will be relocated from around the door and move them to the trash, your car and other parts of the house. You are likely to find that paper is easier to handle now that you've cleared the rest of the room.

18. **DO NOT start making decisions** about single pieces of paper, unless that's all you have to deal with. If you start there, you will quit! Handling big chunks of paper first will

allow you to see visible progress quickly. That is essential in order for you to stay motivated and keep going.

19. **Start by pulling big chunks of paper from your paper piles first**, like magazines, catalogs, newsletters, and stapled chunks of paper. Making decisions about big chunks allows you to see visual progress more quickly than starting with single sheets of paper. Visual progress is imperative to keep you motivated to continue working on paper.
20. **Work your way from big chunks to single sheets**, and then to small pieces of paper.
21. **Keep only those papers you are highly likely to reference at some later date.** Remember, 80 to 90% of paper that is filed *never* gets touched again.
22. **Be very selective about papers you keep**. If you keep them, they become work, because you'll need to figure out how to store them, so you can easily access them.

Keep in mind that the energy in your home office will be *much* improved once you have cleared it of clutter. You will then need to organize your paper and set up a filing system, if you don't already have one.

After all that hard work you can turn your attention to other fun activities, like decorating the space and enhancing it with lovely art and images that bring you joy, create feelings of empowerment, and motivate you to take action.

> **Now that you've read through the steps,
> it's time to apply your knowledge.
> Are you ready to love your home office?**

CHAPTER 6

Living Room/Family Room

*"My favorite room in the house is the living room. We have
two big couches, six recliners and over 20 pillows. It's a
really comfortable place to hang out with my family."*
—Cody Linley

There are typically two kinds of "living rooms": the formal living room and the family room. Energetically they are two very different spaces. The formal living room is often an orderly space holding some of the best furniture and family treasures. Because of the value of its contents, it can have a more formal energy than a family room and is often off limits for children and play.

A family room is just that, a place where family congregates to watch TV, relax and enjoy time with each other. Furnishings are usually chosen for comfort and typically are more casual than the furnishings in a formal living room. This room usually holds things for entertainment, like stereo equipment, DVDs, music CDs, games, books, magazines and catalogs.

From an energy perspective, a formal living room is usually a more peaceful place to be, because it usually does not house high energy items like TVs, magazines, catalogs, CDs and DVDs. The challenge with this formal room is to make sure you've made it comfortable enough to attract people into the space on a regular basis. When not used, its overall energy stagnates and can become negative.

The challenge of most family rooms is to keep them clear of clutter. As a high-use spot in the house, they can become drop spots for paper, book bags, newspapers and magazines. Also, if not stored out of sight, the energy of items associated with entertainment can be quite noisy. Scattered CDs and DVDs and unfinished craft projects and homework assignments can add an irritating energy to the space.

Whether you have a single living room, a living room and a family room, or just a single great room (family room on steroids), keeping those spaces clutter-free and feeling good is an on-going challenge. In this section, I refer to family rooms, but the information can also be applied to a formal living room, if you happen to have both in your home.

Family Room

Family Room: The Second Heart of Your Home

I have described the kitchen as the "heart of the home," the place where everyone gathers for sustenance and connection. The family room is the second heart of the home. Its condition, how it feels, and how it's arranged can have a direct effect on family interactions. A lovely, clean, uncluttered family room that is a warm, welcoming color and has comfortable furnishings will support pleasant exchanges and positive

Living Room/Family Room

interactions among family and friends. Negative energies can induce negative behaviors, irritation and conflict.

Determine the Function of Your Family Room

Most family rooms are used as a place to stop, relax, watch TV, read, play games and enjoy being with family. It's a public area in the home, and a place where activities occur. You have the opportunity to choose whether the space will have a completely restful energy, have a more active energy, or a mix of restful and active energies. YOU make that choice when you decide the functions of your family room.

For example, my family room is almost completely devoted to quiet activities like reading, watching TV, and conversation between my husband and me. We once had a mini-trampoline in the room, that it eventually became a dog bed. If we had decided to activate the mini-trampoline, we'd have added an active energy to the space. The functions of the space would then be rest, relaxation, reading, conversation and exercise; a mix of restful and active energies.

Take a minute and think about the activities that typically go on in your family room. Are you satisfied with what happens in that space? Would you prefer it to be a more restful space? Or, would it make sense to add a computer table and computer to the space, so family members could use the computer and still be accessible for conversation and interaction?

Once you've decided the functions that will be housed in your family room, you'll be ready to begin the clutter clearing process. Your clarity about the types of energy you want to have in your family room will determine the types of items that will be housed there and those that will be removed. What you choose will affect family interactions. You choose; a restful haven or an active area for exercise, computer activities, and game playing . . . or both!

How to Ensure Peace in Your Family Room

A cluttered room, regardless of its furnishings and paint color, is a noisy, stressful environment whose negative energy will have a negative effect on the energy of its occupants. Conflicts are more likely to occur in a cluttered space.

When you think about your family room, do you sigh with pleasure or groan with displeasure, irritation or overwhelm? Family rooms are gathering spots, high use areas for relaxing at the end of busy days and busy weeks. As such, they tend to attract all kinds of things that have very little to do with relaxing, like computers and other forms of technology, CDs, DVDs, newspapers, magazines, catalogs, toys, art supplies, paper. . . the list goes on! If your family room is cluttered, you are not alone! Family rooms seem to take on a life of their own, especially when more than one person is sharing that space.

Guidelines for a Peaceful Family Room
- **Remember that everything is alive with energy, and that the energies of items talk to you all the time.** The more items you have in the space, the noisier the space will be.
- **Keep small items like CDs, DVDs, art supplies and games contained and out of sight** to quiet their noisy energies.
- **Limit the number of knick-knacks** you have out and visible to just a precious few.

Living Room/Family Room

- **Have a balance between large objects (furniture) and small objects (knick-knacks, lamps, etc.)** in the room, erring on the side of more large objects and fewer small objects.
- **Keep paper out of the family room.** If you bring paper into the room to read or work on, be sure to remove it when you leave. Paper usually has the energy of activity and work, and is not conducive to the function of peace and relaxation of a family room.
- **Limit the number of framed photos to one to three per surface** so each photo can be easily seen and enjoyed. Large quantities of framed photos on a surface have the energy of a crowd, often more annoying than pleasurable. Because the energy of a crowd can feel overwhelming, it's less likely that all the photos will be seen.
- **Contain your magazines and catalogs to one or two baskets or bins.** If a basket fills up, consider it a sign that it's time review its contents and let some items go to recycling or the trash.
- **Keep side tables clear by using small boxes to contain small items** that are frequently used in the family room, like nail clippers, nail files, pens, note pads, etc. When those items are used, return them immediately to the box.
- **If you have more than one remote, devote an attractive container to house the remotes.** Return all remotes to it at the end of each day.
- **Teach children that whatever they bring into the room must leave it when they leave the room,** like book bags, school supplies, books, snack wrappers, plates, shoes, iPods, tablets, laptops, etc.

- **Return the room to order each time you leave it** by returning magazines to their basket, removing newspapers, returning dishes to the kitchen, and putting games, CDs and DVDs that were used back in place.
- **Keep the room clean.** Dust and dirt have negative energies. Negative energies can induce negative behaviors, irritation and conflict.

It takes just minutes per day to maintain peace in a family room. Unfortunately, a peaceful family room can also be trashed and transformed into a chaotic mess in a matter of minutes of thoughtless action. Choose for peace!

Family Room Dilemma: Noise Clutter

Electronics have made their way into our lives, adding new dimensions to communication and entertainment. In this day of electronics everywhere, you may find that your family room is anything but the peaceful haven that you want it to be.

Electronic devices have brought new noise into the family room. Where once the TV was the sole source of noise, you now have cell phones with bells and chimes for incoming text messages and emails, tablets and laptop computers with their many sounds, and noisy gaming devices. Even if no one is talking on their cell phone and the TV is off, each piece of electronic equipment has an active energy of its own. Plus, there are the wires associated with each device. Wires have an irritating, negative energy.

Consider the function of the room. Since the primary function of

Living Room/Family Room

a family room is as a gathering place for rest, recreation, and connection with others, its comfort level will be determined by how well you manage the electronic noise in the space. While the array of electronics can enhance communication outside of the home, and add pleasure to our lives, the very presence of those items out in the open in your family room adds an active, sometimes irritating energy to that room. It's best to store them out of sight when not being used. For example, get your laptop out when you're ready to use it. When you're finished, pack it back in its carrying case or put it away in your home office.

iPods and cell phones can be stored in purses or backpacks. Or, set up a docking station for charging all your electronics, which will quite naturally relegate them to just one area of the room.

Next, explore ways to manage all the sounds that interfere with your quiet enjoyment of a cup of coffee while you read the paper. Some TVs have jacks that can allow one person to listen to the TV with headphones, while another reads a book. Or, you may want to negotiate with other family members for quiet times, when the TV and other electronics are shut off.

Get conscious of your noise clutter and take steps to manage it so the family room can be a place of positive connection and enjoyment instead of a noisy, stressful place to be!

How Do You Solve the CD/DVD Dilemma?

Feng shui teaches that everything is alive with energy and that energy talks to you. The greater the number of things you have in a space, the more conversations are going on, and the "noisier" the environment.

Let's look at CDs and DVDs through feng shui eyes. Picture a stack of CDs or DVDs. Each item has its own energy, so essentially a stack of CDs or DVDs is a stack of different conversations going on at the same time. CDs and DVDs are noisy items energetically! Plus, jewel cases of CDs and DVDs, however creative their covers, are not particularly attractive. Having those items out in the open in a room that is intended for rest and relaxation is really at cross purposes with the function of the family room. Yes, family rooms are places for entertainment, but I have a hunch you'd rather do it in a space that is relaxing, peaceful, and attractive.

But, you say, "My music and movies are important to me! The family room is where I use them!" Ok, fine.

Following are a few ideas for reducing the "noise" of CDs and DVDs in your family room:
- **Reduce the volume of the "noise" by reviewing each CD and DVD** to make sure it is still something that you love and intend to play in the future.
- **Replace all broken cases.**
- **Get rid of any CDs and DVDs that are scratched beyond repair.** They hold the disturbing negative energy of brokenness.
- **Remove any CDs and DVDs that are more often used in another location** in your home (e.g. children's playroom or bedrooms).
- **Separate CDs from DVDs and clump each by category.** For example, CD categories might be jazz, country, classical, rock. DVD categories might be children's movies, romance, action/adventure, dramas, musicals, comedy. When CDs and DVDs are organized by category, they take on the energy

of their category instead of each having its own unique energy. Because there are a smaller number of categories than individual CD and DVDs, creating categories quiets the overall energy of each individual item.
- **Store CDs and DVDs out of sight in a cabinet, drawer or storage cabinet** designed for that purpose.
- **Instead of using jewel cases, consider storing CDs and DVDs in CD/DVD binders** designed to hold large numbers of CDs/DVDs. That will reduce the number of items associated with CDs and DVDs, therefore reducing conversations.

When your CDs and DVDs are all gathered in one place and neatly organized in your family room, not only will you have lowered the volume of their noisy energy, but you'll also find you're more likely to use them.

Is It Okay to Have Paper in Your Family Room?

Paper in a family room or living room is a big No-No! Think about the primary functions of a family room: rest, relaxation, social interactions, entertainment, and reading. Paper is work. It's work to decide if you need to keep it, work to take action on it, work to file it if you keep it . . . the list goes on! Work energy and relaxation energy are polar opposites. Why pollute your family room with paper?

When I refer to paper, I'm talking about loose papers; not magazines, catalogs, and newspapers. While magazines, catalogs and newspapers made of paper they usually have very different energies than sheets and scraps of paper. The family room or living room may be the best place to take time out and catch up on the news or peruse a magazine. However, be ruthless with yourself about purging those more appealing sources of paper. Give yourself a deadline for how long you'll keep newspapers, magazines and catalogs. Then, honor it!

If you decide to do some paperwork in the family room or living room, perhaps because it is a more comfortable place to work than your home office, be sure to take the paper out of the room when you're finished working on it for the day. If you leave it behind, even for a few minutes, it is likely to attract more paper, and you'll soon have a paper nightmare in your cozy haven. Or, it will grow roots, making it harder and harder to address and remove as time goes on. Old paper is more difficult to tackle than fresh, new paper. Why? The energy of paper goes dead very quickly. As its energy dies, it becomes more and more negative, making it harder to deal with and move along.

Make your family room and/or living room a paper-free zone (free of loose papers and scraps of paper). Doing so is one of the best ways to ensure peace and peaceful interactions in that important gathering place.

How to Enhance Your Family Room

All clear? Once you've finished clearing clutter from your family room or living room, it's time to have some fun with your creativity! It's time to enhance the space! When you clear clutter from a space, you remove sources of negative energy. When you enhance a space, you intentionally add color, light, and objects, etc. that will increase the positive energy in the space.

Living Room/Family Room

Following are some ideas for enhancing your family room or living room:

- **Make sure the walls are a comfortable color, not white, pastels, black or a shade of red.** Walls that are white or pastel colors (which communicate as white) should be avoided, because they make spaces feel cool and impersonal. Also, we are nurtured by color. The color in your paintings, prints, and other wall hangings does not show up against white walls. Your luscious blue cushions and brilliant floral prints will lose their zing in a white environment. Shades of red are generally too hot for a gathering place. An overabundance of red can stimulate irritability and conflict between family members.

- **Light sources are always an enhancement if in good repair.** Make sure there are at least three indirect light sources in addition to overhead lighting. Pools of light make a space feel cozy. Avoid fluorescent lighting because it is not full-spectrum lighting, and its buzzes and popping sounds, which you may or may not hear, are stressful to the nervous system. To make sure you have adequate lighting, consider having one "up-light," a lamp that throws light toward the ceiling. Also choose lamps that allow 100-watt bulbs. Light is energy. Bright light is high energy. Dim light is low energy.

- **Plants are another great way to enhance your family or living room.** Add live or silk plants to bring the outdoors inside. If you have a black thumb, don't like the look of plants, or don't want to have to maintain them, be sure that you bring in the color of "plant green" with your window coverings, art, pillows and/or throws. Even a small touch of plant green can immediately shift the feeling of a family room or living room from a man-made, impersonal space to a comfortable space. If you use silk plants, be sure to keep them clean. Most silk plants can be cleaned by simply rinsing them with water.

- **Add touches of color to the space with art, window coverings, rugs, objects, pillows and throws.** A painted wall is an expanse of color that has a major overall effect on the feel of the room. Touches of color, like the red spine of a book, yellow daffodils in a painting, and the blue background of a patterned fabric used for draperies, add pops or touches of energy that can transform a room from a blah space to a space that feels so good you hate to leave it. Have fun with color! Treat the room like a canvas upon which you are painting a scene that feels as good as you want interactions between family members to feel.

- **Choose art with themes that complement the types of activities you want to occur in the room.** For example, if you want the space to be a quiet, restful space where you can rest and relax, choose a peaceful landscape or beach scene. Or, if you want the room to be a place for more active family interaction like game-playing and energetic conversations, choose art with scenes of people enjoying time together in sports or dining out. Remember, the theme of a work of art is alive with energy. Add art with a peaceful theme, and you're adding peaceful energy to your space. Add art with a war scene, and you'll be adding the energy of conflict to your space. Choose carefully when adding art. Make sure the energy of each piece is in alignment with your desires for

Living Room/Family Room

the types of activity you want to have happen in that space.
- **Add decorative objects that you absolutely love.** Make sure that each one is either a luscious complement to the rest of the room or has a positive association, like an item that belonged to a special family member, was a gift from a special friend, or reflects a family member's passion (for example, dog statues for a dog lover).

Enhancing you family room is an ongoing process. Ideally your enhancements will change as you and your family change. Plants come and go. Books hopefully get read and then moved out of the space. Decorative objects change as tastes change and new, special items come into your life. Art gets changed out when it fades or no longer speaks to you in the same special way. When you keep your enhancements dynamic and current, you will ensure that you're making positive energy investments in keeping your family room or living room a place for positive experiences.

How to Bring Life Back to Your Living Room

If you ask people which room in their house gets used the least, many will tell you that it's their formal living room. Why? For many people it's the room with all the treasures that as a child you learned was off limits. It was kept nice for those rare occasions when family visited or for Thanksgiving and Christmas gatherings. The living room may also be avoided because its formality makes it less comfortable. When you are ready to relax, the last thing you want to do is spend time in a room you're afraid you'd mess up with dirty shoes, snack plates, dog hair, etc.

From Cluttered to Clear in Just One Year

As nice as it would be to continue to have a showcase room, one that always stays lovely, neat, clean and organized, from a feng shui perspective it's not optimal to have any one space that is not regularly used. The energy of the space becomes stagnant when there is no activity in it. Because the energy of your home affects what happens in your life, stagnation in the living room is affecting some part of your life. For good feng shui, and to attract good into your life, it is ideal to have life-giving, active energy in all parts of your home.

So, how can you reactivate the energy of a living room? Here are some suggestions:

- **Make the living room the place where you meditate or spend time alone every day** reading inspirational and spiritual books.
- **Add a music source,** like a stereo, radio, a special speaker for your iPod, or a Bose stereo system, and regularly turn it on to draw yourself into the room and activate the energies of the room with the sound of music.
- **Keep a vase of fresh flowers in your living room at all times.** Fresh flowers add life to the space and can attract your attention to remind you that the living room is a lovely space to spend some time reading, writing notes, or meditating.
- **Designate the living room as the place where you and your spouse share a cup of coffee or tea** on the weekend and converse about the events of your week, your plans for the future, your hopes and dreams.
- **Add green plants to bring the outdoors inside** and give you a reason to come into the room when they need watering. Don't consider this option if you have a black thumb or if

Living Room/Family Room

you know you'll have difficulty remembering to tend to the plants. Dead plants are <u>not</u> good feng shui!

If the above suggestions about how to use the prime real estate of the living room don't appeal to you, consider giving the space another identity. Some families make their formal living room a playroom for their children while they are young. It becomes the central location for storing toys, books, and games, and is furnished with small tables and chairs, beanbags, and paint easels. Others convert the living room into a home office. This is a particularly appealing option when one of the occupants runs a home-based business.

What can you do to bring your formal living room back to life? Perhaps a new paint color and rearranging the furniture will make the space more appealing and motivate you to make a conscious effort to spend time there. Remember, it's good feng shui to have a living room that is used and loved with regularity. Its energy affects your energy and your life!

From Cluttered to Clear in Just One Year

Family/Living Room Clutter Clearing Plan

Before you begin clearing your living room and/or family room, identify all the functions of each room. That will prepare you to easily identify things that clearly don't fit the function of each space.

1. **Determine the function of the room.** Possible functions for family rooms and living rooms include: entertainment (TV, games, etc.), reading, rest, computer operations, socializing, meditation (usually in peaceful living rooms) and family interactions.
2. **Take a "before" photo of the space.** As you look at the photo, what do you see that makes you cringe, groan or want to run screaming from the room? Those hot spots are negative energy pockets that your clutter clearing will hopefully address.
3. **If you have paper scattered around the room, gather it up (without reading it!), and set it aside in a bag or box.** As stated earlier, if you start with paper first, you're very likely to quit! Paper has an annoying, noisy, distracting energy that talks to you, often saying nasty things like, "What's wrong with you that you can't get a handle on me?" Gathering it up silences those conversations. You will address the paper at the end of the clutter clearing process. Resist the urge to look at every page you're scooping up unless there is some paper you must find for a particular reason. Reading papers as you go is a great way to distract yourself from the task at hand and waste precious clutter clearing time.
4. **If there are lots of small things scattered around,** like pieces

Living Room/Family Room

of toys, earrings, coins, pens, buttons, etc., also gather them into a container or containers and set them aside. They too will be addressed at the end of the clutter clearing process.

5. **Look for large items that can immediately be removed from the room.** Removing them will free up energy that is then available to you, and will help you see progress and feel motivated to continue clearing.

6. **Look around the room and take note of anything that someone living in the home hates.** To facilitate positive interactions among family members, public areas like living rooms and family rooms should not contain any item that someone in the family dislikes. If one person hates something, but another loves it, remove that item from the room and relocate it.

7. **Next, remove any items that you dislike or that don't fit the function of the space.** Place those items close to the door of the room, either inside or outside of it. Don't leave the room until you've made significant progress, you start tripping over items that are slated to leave the room, or you experience brain fatigue from decision-making. When you do leave the room to remove items, take the items to the location where they belong and immediately return to work in the family/living room. Resist the urge to put them away in their new locations. If items are not easily put away, you could be distracted from your goal to clear clutter from your family room or living room by the desire to re-organize the new homes of items that you've moved.

8. **Evaluate all furnishings for comfort, condition and size.** It is especially important that sofas and chairs in a family

room be utterly comfortable. If they aren't comfortable, they won't be used. Whenever possible, position the chairs and sofas that get used most often in the power position, having a solid wall behind them and a full view of the door. People feel most comfortable in the power position. Also make sure that each piece of furniture is in good condition, because the energy of each piece of furniture affects your energy and the energy of interactions between family members and friends. Make sure the size of each piece of furniture not only fits the scale of the room, but also fits the people using it.

9. **If you have piles of mixed items in areas of the room, start sorting piles that contain large items.** Pull the piles apart and sort their contents by category. I call this process "clumping." For example, clump CDs with CDs, office supplies with office supplies, clothes with clothes, and books with books. Once a pile is sorted, decide whether that type of item will remain in the room. If it will stay, leave it where it is. If it belongs in another area of the house, or will be donated or trashed, place it just inside or just outside the door to the room. Resist the urge to leave the room to put things away in other parts of the house! Put away items that will remain in the space, if there is space for them. If not, set the clumped items to the side and continue clearing. You can circle back to those items after all clutter has been cleared and re-evaluate what you are keeping, rethink your storage space, and containerize objects.

10. **Evaluate all light sources.** Ideally family rooms and living rooms have at least three incandescent light sources in addition to overhead lighting. Ideally you want to love

Living Room/Family Room

all your lamps. Consider them 3D art in the space. Ask yourself, "Do they add to the decor or detract from it? Do they provide good light?" If they are old and outdated, let them go! It is possible to find affordable lamps at thrift stores and places like Home Depot, Lowe's, Target, and Walmart. Don't live with lamps you hate! Remove lighting that gives off a harsh light. Also, avoid fluorescent lighting. It is not comfortable lighting because it is not full spectrum, and its subtle buzzing and popping sounds irritate the nervous system. Remove lamps that are fire hazards because they have old or faulty wiring.

11. **Check out the quality of your storage containers.** Is your CD holder attractive and easy to use? If it's difficult to put CDs away, you won't do it, and CDs will pool around the holder. Is the basket or bin that you use to hold magazines in good condition, and is it easy to access when you want to find a particular magazine? Does your storage container for dog toys fit into the space available, or would a smaller model work better?

12. **Next, look at your bookshelf and books.** If you have a book shelf, is it in good condition and attractive? Take a look at the books it holds. Are all the books on the shelves still alive with energy? In other words, is their content relevant to you at this time? Check out all the titles to identify the books that still interest you. Donate those that do not. Do the books reflect past interests and passions that are no longer relevant? If so, let them go. If you have reference books, do you actually refer to those books at some time during the year? If not, consider releasing them. Is the content of your

books uplifting or primarily focused on war, conflicts, and sad subjects? Keep in mind that the content of each book holds that energy of its subject in place in your family room. Those energies affect the overall energy of the room and, in turn, can affect the interpersonal interactions in the space. Keep only those books that hold energies that are in alignment with your current interests and values.

13. **Evaluate all your catalogs and magazines.** If you have multiple copies of one magazine or catalog, lighten your load by recycling at least half of them. Make that happen by letting go of magazines that are older than two months, catalogs that are outdated, and multiple catalogs from the same vender. Remember, you will almost always get another catalog. Also, remind yourself that it's highly unlikely that you will actually go back and read magazines that are over two months old. Plus, magazines will continue to pour in, so you'll never lack for something to read!

14. **Eliminate newspapers older than the current week.** News gets old quickly. Besides, news can be read online, so you needn't worry about missing important articles. Accumulated newspapers can have a dirty, nagging energy, telling you that you are not keeping up with what's happening in the world. Keeping those newspapers could be more detrimental to the peace of your family room than any benefit you might experience if you keep them.

15. **When you've made your way around the room and have evaluated everything except the paper and small items,** it's time to address turn your attention to those tiny objects that you corralled at the beginning of the clutter clearing

Living Room/Family Room

process in the family room. It's pretty normal to easily feel overwhelmed, because each item requires a decision. Again, as in any clutter clearing project, deal with the largest items first. Clump like items together. If possible, make decisions about the clump of items rather than about each individual item. For example, you might have a collection of tiny toy parts. After you group them all together, you realize they all go to a toy that was long ago donated to a charity. Therefore, all those parts are no longer of any use. You can toss them all in the trash! Only when you've finished clumping and clearing out items you no longer need, or use should you move the piles of clumped items to their permanent homes.

16. **Clear paper last.** Now that the rest of the room is clear, tackling that paper will be so much easier than if you had tried to do it early on in the clearing process. Just remember to address the big chunks of paper first. Keep only those papers that are still alive with energy, preferably positive energy. In other words, they will be used by you to take action or referenced at a later date. Remember that 80-90% of all paper that's kept will never be touched again. Once you've cleared out papers you will never use or reference again, move papers to your home office or whatever space you use for paper processing, filing and storage. The family room/living room is not a good place to have papers. Loose papers in a family room/living room hold "work" energy which interferes with rest, relaxation and enjoying time with others.

17. **Be sure to take a picture of your clutter-free family room** and celebrate your success!

From Cluttered to Clear in Just One Year

CHAPTER 7

Utility Room

"Life is too short to fold fitted sheets."
—Unknown

"Utility Room" Does Not Have to Equal "Ugly Room"

When was the last time a family member or friend proudly showed you their newly remodeled utility room? It's very unlikely that you've ever had that experience. Why? Because people don't think utility rooms deserve the same type of care and attention that living rooms, kitchens and even bedrooms do. If you have a gorgeous utility room, you're probably wondering how I have the nerve to express such a strong opinion. Well, I've seen a lot of utility rooms in my years working as a professional organizer, and the decor in a majority of those rooms had been neglected or not even considered. **Most were dingy, nondescript, and boring!**

From Cluttered to Clear in Just One Year

Let me describe the typical utility room I encounter. The walls are white with lots of scuff marks and devoid of art. The room is cluttered with clothing, cleaning products, recycling and other miscellaneous things that were dumped in the space. There are brooms and mops flopping around in a pool of buckets, baskets and other containers. **If that description sounds familiar to you, I can help.**

I have a hunch that the reason the utility room is so often neglected is because it is usually considered a work space. For some reason, work spaces don't seem to count in our culture . . . at least not in the decorating department! Why decorate a utility room or, for that matter, any utility area in your home? One very good reason to decorate utility areas is because the energy of that space the overall energy of the home. A second reason is because you spend time there on a regular basis. Its energy affects your energy! Wouldn't it be a pleasant laundry experience if you were working in a cheery yellow space with special photos of family members on the wall? Heck, you could even use luscious art and window coverings to seduce yourself into facing the boring and dreaded task of doing laundry!

If you have one of those ugly, boring utility rooms, rescue it from the bottom of the list of decorating priorities in your home. In this section, I'll share ideas clearing clutter and for enhancing utility rooms. I'll share ways to transform that utilitarian space into a room you're more likely to treat with the respect and care it deserves.

Utility Room

Utility Room Functions: From Laundry to Cat Boxes

Whether you have a utility room or a utility closet, the first thing to do when you begin clearing clutter from it is to determine the function of the space. For example, my utility room serves as the laundry room, the location of pet supplies like food, cat litter, leashes, and grooming tools, the location of the first aid kit, the location of the cat box and the storage area for household cleaning supplies, vases, light bulbs, and batteries.

As you can see, utility rooms are multi-function rooms. Rarely is a laundry room just for laundry! Because utility rooms are multi-function spaces, they can be a challenge to organize and keep organized!

Following are some possible utility room functions:
- Laundry and laundry products area
- Pet food and pet supplies storage
- Cat box location
- Cleaning products storage
- Cleaning tools storage
- Vases and flower arranging products storage
- Light bulb storage
- Battery storage
- Cord storage
- Recycling storage area

I recently helped clear out a utility room that was being used for both laundry and as a mini-home office. Both functions, home office and laundry, were mixed together throughout the room, creating a disconcerting, uncomfortable energy. What a mix of divergent energies! My first thought was "This just feels wrong!" Soap and paper together? Nah!!!! The first thing I did was separate the paper and office supplies from the laundry items. Having established boundaries between the two functions, the room felt much better.

The above laundry room was unique. I've never before encountered a home office/laundry room combination. But, anything is possible in a utility space! The important thing to do is to make conscious decisions about the range of functions you plan to accommodate in the space. When you do this, you will be able to easily identify objects landing there that don't fit those functions and need to be moved elsewhere. When you don't identify the functions of a space, especially a complex utility space, you are unconsciously laying the groundwork for a disorganized dump. Then you'll struggle to find what you need when you need it, and you'll have more difficulty getting anything done in the space.

Once you've decided the functions of the space, be sure to identify specific locations within the space for each function. As much as possible, work to keep items associated with each function separate from each other. For example, I have one cabinet for paper products for entertaining and another for cleaning products and tools. I have two shelves in a cabinet for pet products. I have another shelf for vases. I don't have enough batteries for a whole shelf, so they are included on the shelf with light bulbs and the box with extension cords. These items all have similar energies and functions.

What are the functions of your utility room? Get clear about what they are, and clear out anything that doesn't fit those functions!

Utility Room

Utility Rooms: Creating Calm in a Practical Place

Utility rooms are usually noisy places. Not necessarily with actual sounds, although that can be the case when laundry is being done. Rather, they are noisy energetically. As you know, feng shui teaches that everything is alive with energy and that the energy talks to you. The more items that are out and visible, the more conversations you have going on in the space. Because utility rooms are multi-purpose rooms, often have open shelving, and house items that don't necessarily fit into cabinets, they can be very noisy places.

Picture this: a utility room with open shelving loaded with cleaning products above the washer and dryer, mops and brooms propped up beside a bucket, and a caddy holding cleaning supplies that can be easily carried around the house when needed. The energetic conversations in that space would be akin to a room full of people talking over each other.

The best way to create calm in a noisy utility room is to first silence as many of the conversations (the broom tells you to sweep the dirty floor, the cleaning products remind you that you need to clean the bathrooms, etc.).

You can do this in several ways:
- Remove any item that doesn't fit the functions of the space.
- Evaluate all cleaning products and pitch those that you've had for several years and never use.
- Add closed cabinets and shelving units to store most items out of sight.
- Organize the items that remain, into categories of like items (e.g. laundry products, pet products, food items, etc.)

- Hang brooms and mops.
- Reduce the number of items left out for convenience to only those you use frequently (e.g. detergent, softener, dryer sheets, etc.).

A utility room that is free of clutter and well organized with most items stored in cabinets and closed shelving units will make your visits to that room much more pleasant and welcoming.

Keep Utility Areas Looking and Smelling Clean

Why is it easier to ignore dirt and grime in a basement or utility room than in a kitchen, living room, or bedroom? Granted, the functions of those spaces are more utilitarian and dirtier. And, hopefully we spend less time in those spaces . . . unless you love doing laundry or woodworking in your basement workshop. But, dust, grime, and dirt in any space feels bad. **Why would you have spaces in your home that feel bad?**

I wonder if part of the reason that many people neglect to maintain cleanliness in the utility areas of their home is because they are unconscious of the fact that dust, dirt and grime are negative energy and ANY negative energy affects the overall energy of their home. Feng shui teaches that everything is connected. What that means is that negative energies in your utility room or basement may be out of sight much of the time, but they still affect you all the time. The overall energy in your home affects what you attract in your life. Negative energies attract challenges and difficulties. Positive energies attract opportunities and good experiences.

What would it take to clean up your laundry room or basement?

Utility Room

Pull out your vacuum, duster, and mop, and make the time to free those spaces of spider webs, laundry detergent spills, and scattered cat litter. Then step back and enjoy the positive energy you've created by cleaning up. I'll bet you'll find that you are less resistant to entering those spaces and spending time there! Cleanliness, even in utility areas, matters!

Utility Room Clutter Clearing: Have Your Cleaning Products Had Babies?

It's always interesting to see how many kinds of silver polish I find when I'm helping clients clear clutter from their utility rooms. I'm not exactly sure how it happens, but I often find duplicates of silver polish, carpet stain removal products, floor waxes, and furniture polish in particular. I wonder if this happens because clients hear about a new, improved product and just have to try it, or if they don't remember that they already have a product. What's also interesting is that when they discover that they have multiples of a product, they want to keep all of them.

I recommend that you figure out which product works best for you, and either let go of the rest or systematically use up the extras. A good way to use up a product is to put the bottle you want to use up in front of the other duplicates. It's also always a good idea to keep smaller containers on lower shelves, so they are visible and easy to access. Even though you use many of those products only occasionally, storing them on an upper shelf guarantees that they will get lost in the bottle jungle. Make them visible and use them up! Also, make a deal with yourself that you will only buy a new cleaning product when you have almost finished using up an old one.

Remember, things that don't get used have a static, dead energy.

And, those extras are taking up prime real estate that could be better used in some other way. Get real with yourself about whether or not those products are really worth keeping! Lighten your cleanser load!

Create a Utility Room You Love

Wouldn't it be wonderful if you actually enjoyed spending time in your utility room? Ok, maybe that's setting the bar a little high. How about having a utility room that you don't dread entering, a room that feels comfortable when you do laundry or look for light bulbs and cleaning products, a room that doesn't push you away with its negative energies?

Once you've cleared out everything that doesn't fit the one of the functions of the space, and have organized those items that do fit its function, it's time to enhance the space. When you enhance the space, you intentionally do things to elevate the positive energies in it.

Below are some of the best ways to enhance a utility room:
- **Paint the walls a color you love**, anything but white or any color that is very light, such as pastel shades, creams, and light tans. Color is energy! It feeds you and nurtures you. Adding the right color can immediately transform the room from a blah, utilitarian space to a space that feels good. When a space feels good, it will attract you to spend more time there. Color also tells you that the room counts. It matters. It's not just one of those rooms that doesn't need decorating. My favorite utility room color is a buttery yellow, specifically "Montgomery White" by Benjamin Moore. But, if you love purple or turquoise, or have identified a shade that would

Utility Room

feel good in that space, go for it!
- **Add visual interest on key walls.** The location will vary depending on the layout of the room, but there is usually at least one wall where you can hang a print, framed photograph, photo collage, or a painting. Use that piece of art as a way to bring more color into the room. Also, make sure that whatever you hang is something that you love. Utility rooms are great places to display whimsical children's art, photographs of people you love, or images of settings you love, like the beach, gardens, or a mountain scene. A utility room is not typically a public room where you would bring your guests, so you can even hang images, art, and sayings of a more personal nature. This might include images that are important to you, but that you don't really want people other than family members to see. I have a shelf over my washer and dryer that I have deliberately not filled completely with cleaning products. I did this so that there will less out in the open and talking to me, and so that there would be open space above the shelf to hang two small cross stitch pieces done by my husband's aunt. I also have one long wall covered with photos and photo collages of special people and animals in my life and a favorite pastel done by my dad. The wall is rich with positive energy. From time to time I change out the images to reactivate the chi (energy) in the space.
- **Add a valance or some other type of window treatment.** Again, you have the opportunity to bring more color into the space with window treatments. Window treatments, especially soft, rounded forms, can bring in a yin energy,

a feminine energy that will balance out the practical, masculine, yang energies of the appliances and other objects in the room.

- **If you have cabinets in the space, have fun by choosing special knobs** that add color a form that is of special significance to you.
- **If you have storage cabinets that don't extend to the ceiling that have room above them, use that space to add a live plant or two or a special decorative object.** Have fun with the space above eye level. If you add positive energy at that level, it can serve to draw your eye up and away from the more utilitarian and often more negative energies of dirty laundry and items associated with tasks that need to be done. I have two such storage cabinets with hearty plants called *pothos* (also called Devil's Ivy) on top.
- **Add a special wall clock to the space,** not a "plain-Jane" utilitarian thing! Search for a clock that you LOVE! For a long time I had a clock I got from a wonderful local gift shop. It had luscious purple and yellow pansies on it. Its garden images were perfect for my utility room, which opens out to my patio and gardens. I moved the pansy clock to my office when I redecorated that space and added a round clock with images of lavender in the utility room. I love lavender. The softness of the lavender images and touches of purple go beautifully with the buttery yellow wall.

Utility Room

Challenge yourself to create a utility room that you just love! Have fun with it! There is no right or wrong, unless you choose to settle for a boring, dingy, dirty, white-walled room. You deserve better! Enhance your way to a room that you'll love!

From Cluttered to Clear in Just One Year

Utility Room Clutter Clearing Plan

Clearing a utility room is not often at the top of "To Do" lists. Why? Because, like the attic, basement, and garage, it's a space with oodles of negative energy, some of which can be dirty and grimy. But, you're now ready to face it! Perhaps you can't stand it anymore. Perhaps you even like the idea of transforming that space into a room that both works for you and is lovely. But, the clutter clearing must happen first. So, here we go!

1. **Start by taking an overall picture of the room,** as well as photos of the hot spots; those areas that are the most chaotic and disorganized.
2. **Take a look at all the different spaces in the room.** Open all cabinets and drawers. Scan the shelves. Note what is stored in each location. Be looking for things that would be easy to throw away or give away (the bigger the better).
3. **Start throwing away those items that are *easy* to get rid of.** Perhaps it's the three extra bottles of floor polish that you've never used and are unlikely to use. Or, you might decide that one stack of rags is all you'll ever need. So, you keep the best and toss the rest. By getting rid of the easy-to-pitch items from any part of the room first, you immediately shift energies from negative to positive and make space to breathe and think clearly.
4. **Go through the whole space looking for the largest items that you no longer need or love.** Move them to an area for trash or for donations, just outside the door of the room.
5. **When you've finished doing that initial clearing, move to**

Utility Room

one area that has items that are large, compared to other items in the room. This could be the floral arranging area that holds vases and bags of Spanish moss, or it could be the cleaning products area. Just be sure you don't find yourself trying to clear tiny things like batteries and buttons. Evaluate each item in that area, asking yourself if you love it or have used it within the last year. If you don't love it and haven't used it, consider either relocating the item to increase the possibility that you'll see it and use it . . . or just lose it! The success of getting one area done will motivate you to keep going.

6. **Make your way around the room, evaluating the contents of each area.** Go from the easiest area to the next easiest area and so on. Many of us don't have strong emotional attachments to cleaning products. That might be a good place to start. Or, perhaps the light bulb and extension cord area is no big deal to assess. Move from easiest to most difficult, and from large items to small items.

7. **If you get stuck, remind yourself that you'll feel so much better when you've restored the space to order and cleanliness.** The negative energy of icky, oozing cleaning products can shut you down. Remember, you really cannot make big mistakes when you're clearing cleaning products and most of the types of items found in utility rooms. They can be replaced! Be courageous! When in doubt, pitch!!!

8. **Reorganize the items that remain once you've cleared an area of items that you no longer want or need.** Begin by clumping like items together: laundry products with laundry products, light bulbs with light bulbs, vases and flower

arranging items with vases and flower arranging items, etc.

9. **Add containers to hold small items that could get lost if left loose on a shelf.** You could have one container for batteries, another for miscellaneous small light bulbs, another for different types of tapes, and another for small, frequently used tools.

10. **Assess whether the current location for each category of items is still the best, given their size and how often you access them.** You may need to shift categories of items around to meet current needs. Make sure to have frequently used items like laundry detergent, bleach, and dryer sheets located within easy reach, ideally no higher than shoulder level. And, always have small items like batteries and small tools located in see-through bins at eye level. Small items are less likely to be used if located above eye level because they are difficult to see. They are also more likely to get disorganized if located above or below eye level.

11. **Keep each category of items separate from other categories.** For example, keep light bulbs separate from vases. They can both be located on the same shelf, if that is the best location for each category, given size and accessibility, but keep each category separate from the other.

12. **Take a final photo to document your success, when you've cleared and reorganized the whole room.** If clutter starts to creep back in, you can use that photo as a reminder of how clean and neat your utility room can be, and how good it can feel.

13. **Keep in mind that this plan is written as if clutter clearing is a linear process. It is not.** It's very difficult to

Utility Room

stay completely on track with the plan. The plan is meant to be a general guide, a reference point to return to when you get stuck or lose your way. If you bounce around while you're clearing and you're still getting lots done, consider it normal. If you bounce around a lot and you're not really accomplishing much, you may benefit from getting help from a supportive friend or a professional organizer.

From Cluttered to Clear in Just One Year

CHAPTER 8

Dining Room

"We have cultural expectations that everyone needs a dining room, yet they're only used three times a year. But if I put a bone handle on the door of an upper-end brick home, I'm making an outlandish statement."
—Dan Phillips

What Is the Function of Your Dining Room?

The obvious function of the dining room is as a gathering place to enjoy a meal. In recent decades, however, with the advent of fast food, the busy schedules people keep, and a shift toward more casual living, dining rooms are less and less often used solely for the purpose of dining. Now, dining in that room may happen only on special occasions like birthdays, Thanksgiving, Christmas and other holidays. The rest of the time, as the room sits in wait for the occasional special meal, the dining room often becomes an annex of the home office with the table becoming a kitchen desk, a sewing and/or craft area or a study spot for children.

Why does the dining room seem to attract the paper that belongs

in a home office or the study materials of children? Because the dining room table is a large flat surface in the proximity of the kitchen. Many kitchens have a postage stamp-sized desk, if they have one at all. Paper lands in the kitchen from all directions: mail, school papers, action items, shopping lists, coupons, menus, etc. It's quite understandable that if the kitchen desk is already overwhelmed or is non-existent, papers would gravitate to one of the nearest flat surfaces.

Some children are not comfortable doing homework in their bedrooms all by themselves. Having people nearby actually helps them focus. The dining room is a perfect place to park themselves to do homework assignments; close enough to the activity of others, but distant enough that a child or children can concentrate on their tasks.

By the way, it's good feng shui to have something happening in every room on a regular basis. Your dining room holds energies that affect your life. It's always optimal to have some type of activity in a space; active energy, as opposed to stagnant/dead energy. Giving your dining room a few additional functions besides just dining could be an energetic asset for your home.

If you still want to use your dining room for dining (even if only occasionally), I recommend that you *do your best to maintain the look and feel of the dining room.* The risk of combining other functions with the dining function is that the room could become a clutter haven, especially if it houses messy functions that involve paperwork or creative projects.

If other functions are added (e.g. studying, bill paying, tax preparation, gift wrapping, art creation, fabric cutting, etc.), then either contain the items associated with those functions out of sight, perhaps in a piece of furniture, or bring in the items necessary to do the activity and clean up and remove them when you're done. Developing the discipline to maintain the dining room as a place where you could enjoy a meal at a moment's notice is an important skill for every family member.

So, what's the function of your dining room? Dining rooms can be beautiful, inviting spaces if they are treated with the respect they deserve.

Why Dining Rooms Become Dumping Rooms

Dining rooms are one of those rooms in many homes that becomes a dumping spot. Why is that?

Here are some possibilities:
- **Dining rooms aren't frequently used** for dining like kitchens or family rooms, so the energy in them stagnates. Stagnant energy attracts stagnant stuff.
- **Dining rooms are often a convenient drop spot**, close enough to active areas to be easily accessed.
- **Because dining rooms often aren't used for dining on a daily basis**, cleaning up right away after working in there doesn't seem urgent or essential.
- **Dining rooms have one large flat surface that is a perfect place to drop incoming items** if you're too tired to put them where they really belong.
- **The dining room table is also a great spot to do projects**, especially those that require a lot of space. More energy is required to clean up after a project than for initiating a project.
- **The dining room is often off the beaten path of traffic through the house.** Therefore, items dropped there are "out of sight, out of mind."

If your dining room has been used as a dumping room, you probably identify with one or more of the scenarios above. Dumping in the dining room is a habit that, like any habit, requires discipline and commitment to change. **If you want to clear the dump and maintain a lovely clutter-free dining room,** identify the causes of the dump and address them. Also make sure that all potential dumpers are on board to break their dumping habits and help maintain a clutter-free space.

Dining Room Associations: Who Is Hanging Out at Your Family Gatherings?

Dining rooms are one of the places in a home where you often find family treasures in the form of inherited furniture, glassware, silverware, serving dishes and china. Have you ever stopped to check out the associations of each piece of furniture and each item in your dining room buffet or corner cupboard? If an item was owned by a family member, it holds the energy of that person. **Therefore, it's as if that person is sharing the space with you every time you enter the room.**

Until recently my dining room held a beautiful sideboard, dining room table, and matching chairs, which my parents had acquired when we moved into a lovely old house in Massachusetts when I was eight years old. Those pieces held the energy of South Walpole, Massachusetts, and our time there. They also held the energy of my family of origin and the many shared meals we enjoyed together, particularly Thanksgiving and Christmas dinners.

Now I have beautiful table that I inherited from my mother and step-father. It holds the positive energy of precious memories of shared meals with Mom and John. The sideboard, which never fit well in my small dining room, was sold and replaced by a lovely dresser with a marble top, which once belonged to an incredible sales and marketing guru who I admire and who I've come to know because for years I was pet sitter for her precious dogs, Gracie and George. The energies of both of those pieces intermingle to make my dining room a warm and lovely place to be.

Inside the dresser are serving dishes and decorative items that belonged to my maternal grandmother, were either given to Bob and me as wedding presents, or were given to me by special friends. Each item holds the positive energy of its previous owner or the giver of the gifts. When I pull those items out, I feel connected to those special people.

Check out who you have residing in your dining room. Their energy could be affecting your energy and the energy of interactions in that room. Make sure that you keep only those things that hold loving, positive energies.

China Cabinet/Dining Room Corner Cupboard: A Haven for Treasures or for Trash?

Have you ever noticed who you have living in your corner cupboard or china cabinet? Not long ago I was helping a man evaluate the energies throughout his house to help him be conscious of them and ensure that they were positive and supportive. He had been divorced for many years, and his feelings about his ex-wife could be described as hostile at best. He was startled to realize that his ex-wife's energy was prominently displayed both inside and outside of his corner cupboard which held their wedding china. Needless to say, we discussed the significance of those pieces and removed them from their prominent location.

The items that are stored in dining room china cabinets, buffets, and corner cupboards are often loaded with associations with family members and past events. That's where we store our "good stuff." Take a look at your dining room storage cabinet; I'll bet you'll find china that belonged to your mother or grandmother, crystal you received as a wedding gift, or candle holders from a dear friend. Rarely does a dining room storage cabinet holds things devoid of associations.

When an item brings back the memory of a family member or friend, it holds the energy of that person. It's as if that person has taken up residence in your space. If the item holds the energy of a significant event, the event will replay in your mind when you see it. Not all events are positive. Check out each item in your china cabinet, buffet or corner cupboard. Pay attention to the thoughts that immediately pop into your mind. If an item has a strong positive association, you could hear: "Oh, I love that! It's the gravy boat we used every year for Christmas," or "That's Nana's salt and pepper shaker set. She was so special." When an item holds a strong negative association, or has no significant association at all, you might hear: "I wonder why that ugly thing was so important to Mom. It belonged to Aunt Thelma, and she was not a nice woman!", or "I don't know where that came from. It isn't nearly as nice as some of my other pieces."

Also pay attention to your energy. Items with good energy are likely to lift your spirits and elicit a warm feeling inside. They often bring a smile to your face. Items that hold memories of painful times or stressed relationships are likely cause your energy to drop and can register as a groan, a feeling of uneasiness, or a frown.

Make your dining room storage cabinets a repository of treasures, not trash. Save items with the best associations, the best energy. Donate the rest!

Dining Room

How to Avoid the "Eat and Run" Dining Room

Want to ensure that your family members gobble down their food and take off before you've even had the chance to have a conversation?

Paint your dining room red, have a great big mirror on one wall and hang a crystal chandelier. Red is a fire element, the highest energy color, and hot and bothersome in large quantities like a wall color. An abundance of red can have the effect of making people more irritable and more likely to get into conflict. Who wants to hang out where everyone is on edge or in conflict?

Both the chandelier and the mirror are energy enhancers as well, stirring up active energies in the space. All that active energy will be felt by everyone in the room, making it hard to sit still, relax and enjoy the food and conversation.

Following are suggestions to create a dining room where people will linger:

- **Avoid red shades in wall color or wallpaper.**
- **Paint the room or use wallpaper that is an earth tone;** tans, browns, buttery yellows, peach (red with yellow and white), salmon (earthy shade of red with yellow), or terra cotta (earthy shade of red with yellow).
- **Avoid large mirrors.**
- **Keep the room clutter-free.**
- **Decorate the room with art of peaceful scenes** like landscapes and seascapes and possessions that hold positive associations with special family memories and/or family members.

From Cluttered to Clear in Just One Year

Transform your eat-and-run dining room into a place where loved ones will love to linger!

Reclaim Your Dining Room Table

One day not long ago, I came back into my dining room after making a phone call. It was the day my assistant was working in my office, so I had taken all my "to do" tasks and spread them on the dining room table. As I looked at the table I thought, "This is what happens to my clients! They need space, so they spread things out on the dining room table." After all, many people only use the dining room table as intended, for eating, just a few times a year! Perhaps because they are not as compulsive as I am, when it's time to do something else, they just leave the things on the table. **Things attracts things, so more things get piled on the table. Then, clearing it seems like a nightmare job**. The energy of the stuff left behind typically is chaotic and negative. And, of course it's normal to want to avoid that . . . unless you are a compulsive neat freak like me!

How many of you having dining room tables that need to be excavated? Does your dining room table bug you? **If it does, bite the bullet and clear it off**. If it takes getting a friend to help you, get it done. You really cannot afford to have large parts of your house feeling chaotic and burdensome. If you have that type of energy in your house, you will attract that type of energy into your life. Besides which, do you want to feel your spirit drop every time you pass the dining room? That's what happens! Also, I'll bet many of you experience a stream of thoughts like, "What a slob you are! Why can't you get that table cleared?" Or, you may hear a nagging voice in your head saying, "You really should clean off that table!"

Dining Room

Once you get the table cleared, make a commitment to keep it clear. You may want to write a reminder to keep it clear and post it on the refrigerator. If you live with other people, make it a family commitment. Let everyone know of the commitment, and ask for their help to keep the table clear. Check it every day. Clear whatever accumulates on it every day. If you clear daily, it won't be a big chore. If you wait more than one day to clear it off, you run the risk of finding that the task seems too big to handle, so you'll go shopping instead.

If you use the table for a project, make a deal with yourself that you will create a new habit of picking everything up at the end of the project. Beware, however, the longer the project lasts, the more likely it is that other things will be dumped on the table. It will also become more difficult to get the stuff off the table. It's as though the papers, tools and other things associated with the project latch themselves to the table with little "energy tentacles."

My preference is to work on a project and pick everything up each day. The evening after my musings about how dining room tables become dumping spots, my dining room table was once again clear. All the bits and pieces of my work were back in my office, and I was able to look at my dining room table and smile.

You may decide that the only way you can keep your dining room table clear is to use it only for its intended purpose, eating. However, you may be worried about how you can change your automatic habit of dumping on that wonderful flat surface. After all, flat surfaces attract stuff. My recommendation is to place either a beautiful flower arrangement (silk is OK) or an ornamental decorative item on the table; something with so much positive energy that it communicates, "Don't dump here!" The item has to be striking, beautiful and big enough to get your attention. When you put it in place, think to yourself, "I don't want anything to distract from this special piece!" Then communicate that thought to family members and ask for their help in keeping the dining room table clear.

Start now. Clear your dining room table in preparation for a special family occasion. Then, commit to keeping it clear all year long. It's a commitment guaranteed to reduce stress and create another peaceful room in your home.

Ways to Give a Stagnant Dining Room New Life

As mentioned in earlier sections, because many dining rooms are only occasionally used for their intended purpose, they become susceptible to being dump spots of things that belong in other parts of the house. Just as a slow-moving stream tends to accumulate debris along its edges, so too does the dining room attract stuff that either has no home or that hasn't been returned to its home.

To prevent debris accumulation in a dining room, **I recommend that if your dining room is to be used as a multi-purpose room, that you intentionally give it several active functions.** If you let your dining room evolve into a multi-purpose room over time, it is more likely to become a mess. If instead you decide it will be a dining room plus the location of the downstairs computer, and art central, you can set it up to accommodate those functions in a way that keeps the room attractive and organized.

A good way to accommodate additional functions in a dining room and keep order and good energy in the space is by making sure that the paraphernalia associated with functions other than dining are primarily enclosed in pieces of furniture, like storage cabinets,

Dining Room

armoires, or chests of drawers. That way the dining room can continue to be a lovely place for a meal, yet can also be used as a space to spread out to do homework, make an arts-or craft project, pay bills, or work on a laptop computer.

My dining room holds the contents of two functions: dining and arts/sewing/crafts. All my art, sewing and craft supplies are stored in two sets of plastic drawers in the corner of my dining room, out of the line of sight from both the front door and the kitchen. When I work on an art, craft, or sewing project, all my materials are readily available. And, when I'm done working on a project, everything is stored away in my plastic drawers. A few oversized art-related objects that don't fit into the drawers are tucked beside them for easy access when needed, and my sewing machine is housed in the hall closet.

If you want to add a computer to the space, I recommend either using a laptop that can be stored in a computer bag in one corner of the room. Or add a desktop computer housed in a tech-friendly armoire, which can be closed when work on the computer is finished. Some families I've worked with have made their dining room "homework central," and use an attractive dresser to hold school supplies. That way, supplies are readily available when children work on the dining room table.

However, you add life to your dining room, **remember that keeping it clutter-free will be an on-going challenge requiring good clean-up habits.** Make your dining room the great workroom that it can be, but also be sure to honor its original function by maintaining order.

Art in the Dining Room

I'll never forget the time I saw a painting of a headless body prominently displayed in the formal dining room of a client. I had just finished my first feng shui training, and was looking carefully at the content of all the paintings I encountered in order to determine whether the content of each painting was appropriate for the function of the space. When I saw that shocking painting, I had to take a deep breath and shut my mouth, so I wouldn't burst out with, "So, this is what people can expect when they eat dinner at your table . . . to have their heads chopped off?" I wisely chose to keep that thought to myself. The content of the painting was so disturbing, both for its inference of potential harm and for its gruesome image, that its negative energy completely filled the room.

When you think about adding art to your dining room, I recommend you consider the kind of welcome you want to give those who dine at your table. Most people want those who enter their dining room for a meal to relax, enjoy the pleasure of their meal and enjoy the company of others. Art that could support that goal would have content that is peaceful, lovely, and a pleasure to view. Good examples would be **gentle landscapes; intimate garden scenes; seascapes; or still life compositions of food, plants or birds.**

Feng shui teaches that everything is connected. The energy of the art, therefore, will affect the energy of the people who gather in the dining room. If you want to encourage people to eat at a leisurely pace and linger over the meal, avoid high energy art that is likely to be stimulating. By high energy art, I mean art with vibrant colors (like strong reds or intense yellows), and strong patterns. That type of art could stimulate passionate conversations, but could also lead to discord and even hasty exits if discussions become too intense.

Scenes that include people engaged in activities or socializing are appropriate for a dining room, as long as the activity is positive, such as two people sharing an intimate dinner together or a crew enjoying a sailing trip on a sunny day. It's best to avoid any subjects that display death, dying, war or conflicts of any kind. Those subjects hold the energy of death, dying and conflict, all negative associations, and could put a damper on positive interactions between diners.

Use your art to set the tone for the types of interactions you want to enjoy in your dining room. Surrounding yourself with art featuring subjects you love, particularly peaceful subjects, is a great way to ensure that your dining room is a place of positive connections; where good memories can be made.

Create a Dining Room for Comfort and Connectedness

When you think of your dining room, you may think of food first. After all, that's why we have dining rooms. They are a place to eat. But, you could eat in front of the TV or in front of your computer. Eating can be done many places. Dining rooms are not just places to eat. They are gathering places, places to bring people together to enjoy a meal.

In "How to Avoid an Eat and Run Dining Room," I offered suggestions about actions to take to create **a dining room where people will love to linger.** In this section, I'll share a few ideas to enhance your dining room to ensure comfort and connectedness among diners.

- **Paint your dining room a comfortable earth tone** (buttery yellow, warm shades of brown, tan, taupe, salmon or terra cotta). Earth tones have peaceful, calming energies that are soothing and pleasant for people in the room.

- **Add touches of color to the room** with art, decorative items, and perhaps bouquets of fresh or silk flowers. Touches of color are energies that bring life to the room and stir up positive interactions among diners.
- **Choose a round or oval table.** The curve of a round or oval table is a friendlier shape than a rectangle. Rectangles have sharp corners that interrupt energy flow between those seated around the table.
- **Check out the associations of each piece of furniture.** Make sure that you eliminate any piece of furniture that has a negative association. For example, if the buffet was inherited from a crotchety old aunt who never had a good thing to say about anyone, sell it and replace it with a piece that either has a positive association or one that you love that has no specific association.
- **Check out the condition of each piece of furniture.** Ideally you want to have only those furnishings that work as intended and have few blemishes. Broken and marred things resonate with a disturbing, negative energy that can affect the energy of people who spend time in the room.
- **Check out the associations of all the decorative items and serving pieces.** If any of the items holds a disturbing association with a particular family member, remove it from the room and consider donating it or gifting it to another family member. Ideally you want to have only items that hold positive associations for everyone who regularly frequents the room.

Dining Room

- **Make sure the type and intensity of lighting in the room is comfortable.** Halogen and fluorescent lighting give off a harsh light and won't be as conducive to relaxation and easy connection among diners. If you don't already have a dimmer switch, add one so you can adjust lighting to a comfortable intensity.
- **Add at least one plant to the room.** The green of plants brings the outdoors inside and immediately makes a room feel more comfortable.
- **Hang prints and paintings of subjects that you and your family love.** Avoid subjects that anyone would find offensive.

Make your dining room a lovely room, and you'll set the stage for creating special memories, comfort and positive connections.

Dining Room Clutter Clearing Plan

As I think about dining rooms I've helped people clear, I've spent the most time in dining rooms that have become drop spots (convenient places to drop things to get them out of the kitchen) or paper places (where paperwork or schoolwork is done). Clearing those types of dining rooms is much more time consuming and much more difficult than clearing a dining room that has not been invaded by items that aren't related to dining. Since the former type of dining room is more problematic, this plan is written to address the "dumped-in" dining room. If your dining room doesn't fit that description, just skip the steps that don't apply to you.

1. **Take some photographs of your dining room.** Examine the photos for hot spots, areas that make you sigh, cringe or want to run from the room. Just notice them, don't judge them.
2. **Decide the functions of the room.** Common functions, in addition to dining, are arts and crafts, homework central, first floor home office/computer area, wrapping station, multi-purpose project area.
3. **Gather all loose papers and put them in bags or boxes and set them aside.** Doing that will help you think clearly and allow for easier decision-making. You will address the papers at the end of the clutter clearing process.
4. **Gather small objects together in a bag or basket** to address at the end of the clutter clearing process.
5. **Look around the room and identify large items that don't fit the functions of the room.** Remove them to just outside

Dining Room

the door(s) of the room. Don't leave the area to put things in other parts of the house until you've worked long enough that your brain needs a break from decision-making or you've accumulated so many things that belong elsewhere that they are impeding your movement.

6. **Examine each piece of furniture in the room.** Do all the pieces fit the functions of the room? Are all pieces in good condition? Remove any pieces that are extraneous or are in poor condition.

7. **Check the associations of each piece of furniture that remains.** If some pieces were inherited from family members or given to you by people you know, they hold the energy of those people. Essentially, you are spending time with those people every time you enter the room. Are you or were you in a good relationship with them? If not, donate or sell those items.

8. **Look at the art in the room.** Check out its condition and associations. Remove any art that is faded, has a dark theme like a storm or war scene, or that holds memories of difficult times or difficult people in your life.

9. **Consider removing large mirrors from the space.** Mirrors are such high energy objects that they can interfere with leisurely dining. If the room serves as a dining room and a work station, however, a mirror could be an asset as an energy enhancer to motivate you to get work done.

10. **Review all decorative items displayed in the room,** such as bowls, dishes, platters, candlesticks, vases, etc. Ask yourself, "Do I love this? Do I use this?" If the answer to both questions is no, consider donating or selling the item, or passing it on

to another family member or friend.

11. **Review the contents of each piece of furniture,** starting with the largest items and working your way to the smallest items. With each item, ask yourself, "Do I love this? Do I use this?" If the answer is no, consider donating, selling or passing the item on to another family member or friend.

12. **Examine the little stuff you collected at the beginning of the clearing process** by using the "Love It, Use It, or Lose It" method. Start with the biggest of the small items and decide if it holds "love it" or "use it" energy. If not, either trash it or donate it. Work your way through all the small items, going from the largest to the smallest.

13. **Sort the paper you gathered up at the beginning of the clearing process.** Sort it into the following categories: papers to keep in the dining room, papers to keep elsewhere in the house, and paper to recycle. See Item 17 of the Home Office Clutter Clearing Plan for additional steps to clear your paper. If paper processing/storage is one of the functions of the room, take the paper you will keep to whatever piece of furniture you have designated to store paper. If the paper really belongs in your home office or some other location in the house, put it outside the door of the room to move later.

14. **Take an "after" photo of your cleared dining room.** Compare it to the "before" picture and pat yourself on the back for all you accomplished.

15. **Plan a celebratory meal** in your newly-cleared dining room!

CHAPTER 9

Guest Room

"An ornament to a house is the guests who frequent it."
—Ralph Waldo Emerson

∽◯

The Holidays Are Coming: Is Your Guest Room Ready?

Some of you probably feel a little panic when you think about what must be done to ready your guest room (or rooms) for holiday guests. Where will you find the time for the excavation that will have to happen to make that room presentable? Why is this likely to be the case? Because, in between guests, your guest room has become a drop spot for the types of things that don't have homes, such as items that belong in the attic (which was too hot to enter during the summer), things you don't want to deal with or don't know what to do with, and/or objects that were stashed there when you needed to clean up the public areas of the house for visitors. Many guest rooms become a wildly disorganized "closet" for stuff that people don't want to deal with in the moment.

Why is the guest room so vulnerable to such mistreatment? It's assigned function is for an infrequent event, having company. Since no particular activity happens in that room on a regular basis, its energy becomes static. Static energy is negative energy. Remember, like energies attract. The static, negative energy of a guest room can attract the negative energy of clutter.

How can you keep your guest room ready for guests without having to schedule an excavation? Assign your guest room specific functions that will keep its energy alive all year long. Read on for a list of possible functions for a guest room.

Guest Room Functions: A Challenge of Competing Energies

These days it's seldom I find pure guest rooms, that is, bedrooms devoted exclusively to the comfort of guests. Instead, they function as a guest room *and* a:

- Sewing/craft room
- Art studio
- Home office/file storage area
- Home-based business office
- Gift/gift wrap storage and work area
- TV or computer room
- Photo/memorabilia storage area and work area

Guest Room

- Bedroom for a snoring spouse or a spouse escaping snoring
- Drop spot

While it is beneficial to have something going on in a guest room between guest visits to keep the energies in that room active, **it can be challenging to combine the restful function of sleep with an active function of work, especially in a home-based business office.**

I'll never forget one client who hired me to help him in his home-based business office because he was having difficulty being productive. Front and center was a double bed. And, as you would expect, that lovely, large flat surface was covered with paper. Having such a large flat surface was one challenge, but the bigger challenge was that the bed screamed, "Rest, sleep!" No wonder he had difficulty being productive! The square footage of sleep space far exceeded the square footage of work space. Those two energies were competing, and "sleep" was winning!

When making your guest room a multi-function room, first think about how often you have guests. Unless you have guests once or twice a month, I recommend you consider replacing the typical double or queen size bed with either a futon, Murphy bed, sleep sofa, or inflatable bed that can be set up when guests arrive and put away when they leave. That way, there's still a place for guests to sleep, and between guest visits, the room can have a more active function without competing with a major sleep energy source like a large bed.

How often is your guest room used for guests? If your answer is "seldom," then consider removing the bed—or at least hiding it—so the room can work effectively for its other more active function or functions. You'll find it much easier to keep the room clutter-free and organized when it has complementary functions (e.g. either all active or all restful) instead of two or more functions with competing energies.

From Cluttered to Clear in Just One Year

The Guest Room: Static or Cluttered

I've often wondered why people devote a whole room to guests. Few people have space to spare in their homes, so why set aside a whole room for guests unless you have frequent overnight visitors? What I've found during my years of helping people clear clutter is that one of two things happen in guest rooms: 1) they become nicely decorated spaces where almost nothing ever happens except occasionally housing guests; or 2) they become a multi-purpose, catch-all room and home for things that don't have a home or things that haven't been put away.

The guest rooms where very little ever happens becomes "dead" spots in the home, places where the energy becomes static. **Rooms tend to have better energy if they are regularly accessed or they are used for some activity fairly frequently.** Because every part of the home holds energies associated with some part of your life, having a dead spot in your home can translate to having less positive energy in some part of your life. For example, if your guest room is in the career area of your house and is rarely used or accessed, you may find that opportunities for advancement dry up or efforts to get ahead are thwarted at every turn.

Guest rooms that become multi-purpose rooms not by design, but by accident, are prone to deteriorate into dumping spots that become havens of negative energy. Once the dumping starts, the negative energy of clutter will attract more of the same. **Have you ever noticed that once you start dumping in a spot it becomes easier to keep dumping there?**

What is a better alternative to static or cluttered guest rooms? In the following section, I'll describe how to intentionally create a functional multi-purpose guest room that will be less prone to becoming a dumping ground and will be alive with positive energy.

Guest Room

Setting Up a "No Dumping" Multi-Purpose Guest Room

The best way to set up a guest room as a multi-purpose room is to identify the functions that will exist in the room and deliberately organize the room to accommodate those functions. As I've mentioned before, guest rooms that become multi-purpose rooms by default, with no real planning and intentional organizing, usually don't work well and are prone to become a disorganized mix of stuff pertaining to several functions.

When you decide to reclaim your dumped-in guest room or to change your single function guest room into a space that can accommodate multiple functions, first start by deciding the functions that will be held in that space. For example, your multi-purpose guest room might be gift central, the place where wrapping supplies are kept and gifts stored, plus a home office and craft area.

Next, decide where the supplies associated with each function will reside. You might decide to store wrapping paper, bags, tape and ribbons in a rolling plastic set of drawers located in the closet. The gifts will be stored in a plastic container on the floor of the closet. You then identify one corner of the room for a filing cabinet and computer station (the home office area), and another corner for plastic drawers filled with craft supplies (the craft area). Larger craft supplies can be stored in the closet. By taking the time to strategically plan the location of each function, you will be creating a structure that defines where items associated with each of the functions will live. When you fail to make the time to plan out the locations of items associated with each function, you give the space permission to melt down into a cluttered mess.

You may find that your system of organization doesn't work opti-

From Cluttered to Clear in Just One Year

mally at first, but the more you use the space and the system, the more you'll discover what works for you and what doesn't, in terms of easy retrieval of items and ease of putting things away. When you find that it's inconvenient to access an item that is needed frequently, make adjustments to your original plan until accessing and putting everything away is easy. When it's easy to do, you are more likely to do it.

Guest Room

Guest Room Clutter Clearing Plan

For some of you, clearing your guest room will be no big deal. It's just a guest room free of dumped stuff. Lucky you! But, that is not always the case. As noted above, the guest room, because it's not used frequently, becomes the victim of stashed stuff that you don't want to deal with. So, clearing a guest room can be more like clearing a mini-attic. This plan is written to help people clear the worst-case scenario guest room. If your guest room is not a dump, just skip the steps that don't apply. Happy clearing! Take a "before" photo to document the space before you start clearing.

1. **If your guest room is actually a multi-function room, first determine the functions housed in your guest room.** Be specific about the activities that you intend to accommodate in that space. If you are vague about the functions, the room is free to become a clutter gathering spot. In addition to the function of housing your guests, other common functions for a guest room are listed above.

2. **If papers are part of the contents of the room and part of the visible clutter, gather them together in boxes or bags and put them aside** to be addressed at the end of the clutter clearing process. Doing this will quiet paper's noisy energy and make it easier for you to think while you work on clearing the room. Resist the urge to read any of the paper while you are gathering it up. That will slow your progress, use up valuable mental energy, and won't produce significant results.

3. **If there are small items scattered around the room, gather**

them up in a basket, box or bag. You'll address them at the end of the clutter clearing process. Like paper, they too have a noisy, distracting energy. Starting with small stuff is a good way to guarantee that you'll shut down, get discouraged and/or quit.

4. **Remove any large items that do not fit the activities that will occur in your guest room.** Removing those items will free up energy that will then be available to you as you continue your work. You'll also be able to see visible results for your efforts and feel encouraged to continue.

5. **Decide how you will accommodate the various activities that will happen in the room.** For example, you may decide that the room will be a combination of "gift central"/guest room/home office. For the "gift central" function, you might decide to keep purchased gifts on the top shelf of the closet, store wrapping and mailing supplies (such as gift paper, bows, tape, and mailing boxes/envelopes) in a transparent plastic set of rolling drawers inside the closet, and place a table nearby for wrapping. For the home office function, you might locate the computer and filing cabinet in one corner of the room. It's a good idea to place the guest bed and dresser on the opposite side of the room from the more active functions. Once you've determined the regions for the various functions of the room, you'll have places to put items associated with each function.

6. **Begin sorting things into categories starting with the biggest items and working your way down to the smallest items.** Have at least one category for each function in the room, one for items that don't fit any of those functions, one

for donations, and one for trash. Put items that fit in the last three categories near the door or just outside it.

7. **Don't leave the room until you've collected a sizable quantity of items near the door, you've worked at least fifteen or twenty minutes, or you've worked until your brain is tired from making decisions.** Then move the items that have accumulated by the door to their appropriate locations; put trash in your outdoor trash cans, donations in your car, and other items in the parts of the house near where they belong. Don't stop and put those items away or reorganize any of the spaces where you take things. Just leave the items near their assigned "homes" and make a mental note that you will need to follow up and put them away later.

8. **Return to the room and begin the sorting process again.** Remember, big things first. Save drawers, paper and small items to sort last.

9. **When everything has been sorted but paper and small items, sort the small items.** Start with the biggest of them and work your way down to the smallest. Ask yourself, "Do I love this? Do I use it? When was the last time I used it?" Pitch anything you don't love or use at least once a year. When you've finished sorting, move items that don't belong in your guest room outside the door of the room to move later.

10. **Once you've been through everything else in the room, sort the paper.** Sort it into the following categories: papers to keep in the guest room, papers to keep elsewhere in the house, and papers to recycle. See Item 17 of the Home Office Clutter Clearing Plan for additional steps to clear your

paper. If paper processing/storage is one of the functions of the room, take the paper you will keep to whatever piece of furniture you have designated to store paper. If the paper belongs in your home office or some other location in the house, put it outside the door of the room to move later.

11. **Organize each of the regions of the room, creating homes for everything.** First clump "like" items together. Then use containers to hold groupings of like items and create a structure that will help maintain order.
12. **Take an "after" photo** and celebrate your hard work!

If you get stuck in any part of the process, be gentle with yourself. Getting stuck could be the result of your brain wiring, and is often not a character defect or a matter of laziness. If you are unsuccessful at figuring out how to get unstuck, ask for help. Some people, particularly those with brain wiring issues, work better with another supportive person.

CHAPTER 10

Basement

"Some men can live up to their loftiest ideals without ever going higher than a basement."
—Theodore Roosevelt

Ways to Approach Basement Clutter Clearing

So, you've decided you really want to clear out your basement. How will you approach that enormous task? After all, wanting to clear a basement and actually getting it done are two very different things! Following are some possible approaches to make it happen.

- **Light a match**—just kidding. This option might be appealing, but is not really a good idea! I don't think insurance covers this approach to basement clutter clearing!
- **Commit to fifteen minutes of clearing one weekend day for as many weekends as it takes to finish the job.** This method is comparable to the way you might approach eating an elephant. If you knew you had to eat an elephant, how

would you get the job done? One bite at a time. You may find you want to work longer, but make fifteen minutes the minimum you will work. Even though the size of the job is still overwhelming, with this approach you at least make the time commitment per clearing session small enough to be doable and reduce overwhelm. The trick to this method is to find ways to keep committing to those small chunks of time week after week. Consider rewarding yourself after a successful clearing session (remember, just fifteen minutes!) with an experience you'd really enjoy. For example, you might take a trip to Starbucks for a cup of coffee while you read the paper or a good book.

- **Block off a weekend and tackle the job head on, with or without the help of family members.** This approach is like diving into the deep end of the pool. It's scary, but you just do it! It can work for people who have the ability to make themselves do things, however abhorrent, because they want the end result: an organized, functional basement. You need to have the ability to keep your head down and not let yourself be distracted by the negative energies of the contents or the enormity of the task. You also need to be able to regroup from time to time, when you feel overwhelmed or mentally fatigued from all the decision-making, or physically exhausted from your efforts to move things around and out of the space.

- **Ask a supportive family member or friend to help you clear your basement in exchange for helping them in some way.** Spend at least two hours working together. Your assistant can help by moving things out of the basement as you identify

Basement

them for donation or trash. Schedule more sessions for this type of help until the job is done. Remember, the person assisting you is just that, an assistant. Make sure you stay in charge of the process. The presence of a supportive other makes it easier to stay focused on the task at hand (if you don't get distracted by chit chat and other activities), and makes this overwhelming task less daunting by becoming a social event instead of an onerous task.

- **Hire a professional organizer and work with her in blocks of at least two hours until the project is done.** Professional organizers know how to approach large projects like clearing a basement. Some can even bring in a team to clear the basement in one or two sessions. Others who are solo practitioners can work side-by-side with you, helping you make decisions about what to keep, what to toss or donate, and how to reorganize the space once it's cleared. When you work with a professional organizer, you're likely to get the job done two to four times faster than you could do it by yourself on a good day. The end result is likely to be organized in a way that (with some effort on your part) is more likely to stay organized over time.
- **Wait for a hurricane to flood your basement and force you to excavate its contents.** Yes, I'm trying to add humor here, but this has actually happened. Clients have shared their stories of this type of clearing following major hurricanes like Fran, Gaston and Isabelle. I don't recommend it because it's pretty traumatic and a nasty, dirty process.

How will you get your basement cleared? It might be helpful to know that the basement holds the energy of your unconscious. The reward for clearing it could be letting go of some old unconscious beliefs that don't support you and/or memories that block positive progress in your life. Make it happen and you'll feel lighter and more grounded in the present!

How to Avoid a Basement Dump

Is your basement a dump? Is it a place where things land when you can't make a decision about what to do with them? Basements are high risk areas for becoming dumps because they are often used as storage areas and they are out of sight of the public areas of the home. Many basements are also energy-challenged because they are below grade, and therefore damp and dark. Somehow, it's easier to dump in places that don't feel good. The negative energies caused by dampness and darkness tend to attract more negative energies in the form of dumped stuff.

The best way to avoid creating a basement dump is to commit to designating the basement a "No Dumping Zone." Let other family members know of the designation, and ask them not to dump things in that space.

If you leave the functions of the space undefined, you're creating the perfect conditions for the formation of a dump spot. Possible basement functions include: storage, man cave, home office, family room, utility room, home theatre, TV area, laundry area, workshop, kitchen annex, playroom and extra bedroom.

Yes, the basement is another multipurpose space, hence the clutter and organizing challenges. Because many basements are open spaces housing multiple functions, with few physical boundaries separating items of each function, it's easy for them to become chaotic places. To prevent clutter and chaos, I recommend identifying areas of the space that will hold items associated with each function. You may want to add screens or partitions to wall off certain areas, or use shelving to create physical barriers between categories.

Once you've set up your basement with distinct "homes" for each function, show all family members what you've done and ask for their cooperation in maintaining the basement as an organized "No Dumping Zone." Then commit to maintaining the order you've created!

Creating a Home Office in the Basement

Basement home offices can seem like a good idea because the space is available. It's also away from the hustle and bustle of daily life. That should make it an ideal place to get a lot of work done, right? Why is it then that I find people who have basement home offices working on the dining room table or the kitchen counter? I suspect it's because the energies in a basement are the lowest in the whole house. In other words, it doesn't feel as good to work in a basement as it does on the first, second or third floors of a house.

What causes the basement to be less comfortable than the rest of the house? Some part of most basements is below grade, which creates dampness and a haven for mold. Windows in basements are often small, if they exist at all, so there is often inadequate natural light. Some basements aren't completely finished, having exposed pipes and ductwork. Others have ceilings that are lower than a comfortable eight feet. We don't feel comfortable underground, and we don't feel comfortable when the ceiling seems to be pressing down on our heads.

I'm sure you're wondering if there are things you can do to improve

the energies of a basement. Yes, you can.
- **Make sure you have abundant lighting**, preferably full spectrum incandescent lighting.
- **Make the office feel comfortable by painting the walls one of your favorite colors.** I recommend a buttery yellow, sage green, terra-cotta or an earthy turquoise. Avoid grays, pastels and shades of white or red.
- **If you have a concrete floor**, you can paint, tile, or carpet it to make it more appealing.
- **Organize and arrange** the space for maximum efficiency.
- **If needed, run a dehumidifier** to remove moisture from the air.

You can do all of those things, but if your home office is below grade with minimal natural light, it's still going to feel like you're working in a cave. Because the activities that happen in a home office require high energy plus lots of attention and focus, both difficult to muster in a cave, it is best to locate your home office on the first floor or above. Then, use cave-like basement areas for low energy functions like storage, doing laundry, or a playroom for kids.

Enhancing a Basement

Most basements have energy challenges. As mentioned above, their energies tend to be the lowest in the house because they are set partly underground and because they usually have small windows that limit light. It's almost impossible to enhance a basement so that its energy is comparable to that of upper floors, but, there are things you can do to

Basement

make your basement feel more comfortable.

- **When possible, finish the walls and ceilings with sheetrock.** The smooth look of sheetrock has better energy than unfinished walls, and exposed ductwork, wiring, and pipes.
- **Paint ceilings white and walls a warm color that you love.** Avoid white and pastel colors for walls because they show dirt easily and feel cool and antiseptic. Instead, choose an earth tone (like a warm tan, sand, terra cotta, or buttery yellow) or a favorite color that you love.
- **Cover concrete floors with tile, carpeting, or some type of laminate flooring** that is attractive and easy to maintain.
- **Add attractive lighting.** Basements need to be well lit to add energy to these low energy places. Avoid fluorescent lighting because it is not full spectrum and it buzzes and pops, irritating the nervous system. If the windows in your basement are small or non-existent in certain areas, you may need to add extra lighting to make the space comfortable enough to want to spend time there. The addition of can-style lights or "up-lights" (lamps that throw light up to the ceiling), particularly in areas that have low ceilings, is particularly important. Light hitting the ceiling is a great way to make a ceiling seem higher and thus more comfortable.
- **Add high energy art:** art with bright, vibrant colors; whimsical compositions; and art with people or animals. The energy of the art can transform a plain, utilitarian space into a space where you want to spend time. Good art also sends the message that the space should be treated with respect. No dumping here!

- **Add plants and items with plant-green colors.** Live plants may not survive the low light of a basement or may be too far away from the center of action in your home to be maintained successfully. Dead, struggling, or dying plants are not good feng shui! If that is the case, use good silk plants that look real. Plants not only bring the outdoors inside, but they soften the hard edges of any utilitarian space. If plants are really *not* your thing, add plant-green colors to the space with furniture fabrics, window treatments, rugs, pillows, throws, or touches of color in your art.

Wouldn't it be wonderful to actually **love** your basement? It really can be more than a storage space or a dump! However utilitarian its functions, enhance it! Its energy affects your energy and the energy of everyone living in your home. Wouldn't you rather it be wonderful? Take some of the steps above and make it so!

Basement

Basement Clutter Clearing Plan

Clearing clutter from a basement is a big project. It's probably underground, and any disorganization generates a chaotic, negative energy that can push all but the most determined and courageous people away. But, you can get the job done if you approach the challenge this way:

1. **Determine the function of your basement.** What activities will occur there, and what types of items will be stored there? My basement in my old house was used for doing laundry, exercising and storing tools and building supplies. Functions could include those associated with a laundry room, workshop, home office, or recreation room. Storage could include bulk items, large occasional-use kitchen items, coolers and picnic supplies, lawn chairs, tools, paints, building supplies and more. Be specific about the function of the space and you'll be less likely to use it as a convenient dump!

2. **Look for large items that are easy to get rid of, so they can immediately go to the trash or the donation box.** Get those things up and out of the space right away. I'm talking about no-brainer items like ancient paint cans, broken furniture that's not worth replacing, bags of clothing you'd planned to donate that hadn't yet made it to your car, stacks of magazines that you'll never have time to read, etc. Moving those things out will free space and energy that is then available to you. It will also cause an immediate shift in energy that will help motivate you to keep going.

3. **Don't start with paper!** If there is loose paper in the space, gather it up in a bag or box and set it aside to deal with at the

end of the clutter clearing project.

4. **Check the whole area for trash.** Gather up anything big or small that can be tossed and throw it out. I'm talking about obvious trash. If you have to deliberate about something, it's not obvious trash. Examples of obvious trash are candy wrappers, dirty paper towels, empty paint cans, broken vases, etc.

5. **Gather up all the small items** like nails and screws and put them in one container to deal with when you have finished going through everything else in the space.

6. **If you find boxes of mixed items and/or papers that you need to go through, clump them all together** to deal with after you've made your way through the whole space evaluating larger items.

7. **If your basement is a jumbled mix of items, and the mix has some big items in it, sort the mix into piles or areas of like items.** For example, extra furniture goes with extra furniture. Paint goes with paint. Tools go with tools. Building supplies go with building supplies.

    Remember, be sure to gather up all the paper (without reading it) and put it aside. Then put aside small items. Don't bother to sort them into individual categories at this point in the clearing process.

8. **Decide what items from those sorted piles you can either throw away or donate.** Once items are clumped it will be easier to see how much you have of each category, making it easier to decide what to keep and what to get rid of. Make sure that anything you keep both fits the current function of the space and fits comfortably in the space. Get rid of

Basement

anything that doesn't fit one of the identified basement functions.

9. **If your basement is not a jumbled mix of items, begin evaluating everything in the space to determine if it fits the current function of the space.** Remove anything that doesn't fit the function. Start with the biggest items and work your way down to the smallest items.

10. **Place items to be removed by the door** to the outside or by the stairs until you have accumulated enough to justify a trip to the trash or, for donations, to your car. Removing items from the space will relieve it of some of its negative energy and make it easier to continue clearing clutter.

11. **When you've finished evaluating everything in the space except the clumped paper, small items, and boxes of mixed items and paper, go through the boxes of mixed items.** Again, be sure to begin with the boxes that contain items that are the easiest to make decisions about, papers mixed objects instead of mixed papers. If some of the boxes have both mixed papers and mixed objects, pull the objects out and evaluate them first. Clump the paper and save it to do last.

12. **When you've finally backed yourself into small stuff and papers, do the small stuff first.** Objects are almost always easier to deal with than papers. Begin with the biggest of the small things or the easiest to get rid of. Make decisions about what to keep, clumping like items as you go: coins with coins, buttons with buttons, toy parts with toy parts, etc. Trash or donate the rest. Remember, anything you choose to keep becomes work because you then have to find a home for it

and move it to its home. Search for diamonds among the small stuff. Be willing to part with the rocks!

13. **Finally, it's time to tackle paper.** Paper will be much easier to face now that the rest of the basement has been cleared and is better organized. Remember to first look for paper that's easy to get rid of, usually slick stuff like catalogs, magazines and junk mail. Also look for big chunks first so you'll be able to see and feel progress quickly. Look for stapled chunks of paper, newsletters, magazines, journals and catalogs. Get rid of those things first, and all those individual pieces of paper will be much easier to evaluate. The basement is generally not a good place to have papers. Unless the boxes of paper are archived documents and tax papers, move papers you will keep to your home office or where you work with and store papers.

14. **Once you are done, take a photo and compare it to your "before" photo.** Pretty amazing, isn't it! Celebrate your accomplishment! Clearing out a basement can be a tough job because of the quantity of clutter that can accumulate in that out-of-the-way place, and because the energies in basements are generally lower than in any other area of the house. Pat yourself on the back and commit to keeping your basement clutter-free from now on!

CHAPTER 11

Garage

"The slogan of progress is changing from the full dinner pail to the full garage."
—Herbert Hoover

How to Create a Clutter-Free Garage

Garages can be overwhelming clutter clearing challenges for homeowners. They hold so much stuff and so many different kinds of things. They also become dumping grounds for things that fit nowhere else. Without careful tending and on-going maintenance, they can become an organizing nightmare of mammoth proportions.

In this chapter, you'll learn all of the following: why it's important to maintain a clutter-free and organized garage, why it's so difficult to stay motivated to maintain an organized and clutter-free garage, where to start your clearing efforts, how to break through your feelings of overwhelm and resistance to begin the garage clutter clearing process, how to bring your garage up to date with your current life, how to create an order in your garage that works for you, how to enhance your garage when it is used as the primary entrance into your home, and how to create good feng shui in your garage.

Your garage doesn't have to be one of the most dreaded spaces in your home, a haven of negative energy. You too can learn how to treat yours as the very important room that it is.

The Condition of Your Garage Affects Your Life

Why should you worry about the condition of your garage?

Feng shui teaches that everything is connected, meaning that negative energy in any part of your home will affect the overall energy of the home. If your garage is attached to the rest of your house, its energy can therefore have a profound effect on the energy of your home.

In fact, every part of your home holds energies of the different parts of your life. What you have in your garage and how it's arranged will affect what happens in that part of your life. For example, if your garage happens to be in an area of the home that holds the energy of wealth and prosperity, broken things in your garage could attract money problems, or "broke-ness." If your garage is located in the love and marriage area of your home, chaos in the garage could make normal marital challenges more difficult to deal with and overcome.

It is not as important that you know the specific part of your life that could be affected by garage clutter, dirt, and grime as it is imperative that you understand that the condition of your garage matters. If it is kept clean, organized, uncluttered and functional, then it will be an enhancement to the overall energy of your home.

If its condition is allowed to deteriorate into chaos and disorder, it

Garage

will be a drag on the energy of your home and your life.

Start thinking and treating your garage as you would any room in your home. Clear its clutter. Organize it. Keep it clean. Then notice how you feel about your garage, your home and your life. A clutter-free, organized garage can be just the enhancement your home and you need!

Garage Clutter Clearing: The Challenge of Negative Energies

If you have a garage you probably have had this type of experience. You or your spouse set your intention that this weekend you're going to tackle the garage. The weekend comes. After your breakfast, coffee and the newspaper, you set out for the garage, fully prepared to take on the beast. You open the door; take a look at the chaos, clutter, dirt, and enormous quantity of items to be sorted and organized; then turn on your heel and quickly return to the comfort of your family room and a good book.

Garages rank right up there with attics, basements, and paper as clutter clearing challenges that are most often avoided. Why is that? With few exceptions, most garages present with a whole host of negative energy challenges. In other words, garages tend to be places that, for one reason or another, don't "feel good." Spaces that don't feel good energetically will push you away. Negative energy repulses. Positive energy attracts.

Following are some of the sources of negative energy in garages:
- **They are typically storage areas of an enormous quantity of items.** The numbers of things to be organized, stored and kept in order is overwhelming.

- **They are also typically very busy places.** Items of all sizes from large yard equipment like lawn mowers and weed eaters to tiny nuts, screws and bolts are stored there. Plus, most of those items are visible. If they're visible, their energy talks to you all the time. There is no peace in the typical garage with all those different conversations!
- **They usually hold various kinds of toxic substances** like fertilizers, pesticides, and paints.
- **They are the storage area for tools that can do harm**, like hand saws, drills, axes, chain saws, hammers and crow bars.
- **They are often unfinished spaces with exposed framing.** Even though it is common to leave garages unfinished, they still feel like spaces waiting for finishing touches to make them more attractive and appealing.
- **Garages are dirty places.** Even with the most deliberate attention to keeping a garage clean, dust, dirt and grime easily accumulate because of its enormous door.
- **Garages are dumping grounds.** They are convenient places to drop things on your way into the house. Also, they generally have room to put things "temporarily" when shifting things around inside your house. If you can't decide what to do with items, or if you run out of room for things in the house, your mantra might be, "Stick it in the garage."

Are you now feeling sufficiently overwhelmed? Don't worry. That's very normal. This monster *can* be tackled. But first it's important to be conscious of the sources of negative energy that can shut you down.

If you head for the garage unprepared for its common challenges, such as the power of its negative energies, you are likely to find yourself on the sofa instead, time and time again.

Once you have an awareness of the sources of negative energy, you can use that knowledge to inform your retreating self that it's the negative energy that is dousing your enthusiasm to create calm in your garage. It's not simply laziness or an inability to do the job. Then you can take a deep breath and, with awareness of the power of negative energy to shut down clutter clearing and organizing attempts, move forward to manage those negative energies so you can reclaim your garage.

Garage Clutter Clearing: Trash First

One way to break through your resistance to tackling an overwhelming garage is to focus on trash. Yes, trash. Don't worry about how to reorganize the space. Don't worry about those items you're not sure you should keep. Just look for things that clearly belong in the trash or at the dump. Moving out trash is a great way to get the process of clearing and reorganizing your garage under way.

In your search for trash, first be sure to look at all the big items in the space. Don't get hung up on nuts, bolts, screws, and small tools. If you do that, you won't see and feel immediate progress, and you'll likely quit. Progress is something you'll need to be aware of in order to stay motivated and continue the job. Once you've reviewed the large items, move to the medium items, and then finish with the small items.

To help you in your search for trash, I've compiled a list of typical garage items that can go to the trash or dump:

- **Broken or damaged furniture** that isn't worth repairing
- **Yard equipment that no longer works** or does not work well

- **Broken yard tools**
- **Broken or damaged hand tools**
- **Broken or damaged power tools**
- **Broken tool boxes** or plastic storage containers
- **Cardboard boxes** that are water damaged or falling apart
- **Old paints** (I've been told that paint over six months old grows mold that affects the color)
- **Old bags of fertilizer**, birdseed or grass seed that have gotten wet
- **Empty bags** of birdseed, fertilizer, grass seed, pesticides
- **Ancient yard and garden chemicals**
- **Old or broken planting pots**
- **Sports equipment** that is broken or in poor condition
- **Flat, popped or worn balls** (footballs, soccer balls, baseballs, basketballs) that can't be rejuvenated
- **Damaged lawn chairs and beach umbrellas**
- **Old shoes** that are no longer worn
- **Expired foodstuffs** (if you use your garage as kitchen overflow)
- **Mystery items**—things you have no clue what they are or how they could be used
- **Anything that has been ruined** by moisture or pest infestation

Load up your trash cans and if necessary, fill your car, van or truck with the overflow trash and take it to the dump immediately. When you get rid of trash you are removing enormous quantities of negative energy from the space. Just getting all those things out will give a huge boost of energy. Then you'll be ready to evaluate the rest of the garage items

Garage

and create a new order. Look for trash first and you'll be on your way to garage clutter clearing success!

Need a Garage Update?

Your garage is a place that tends to accumulate stuff over the length of your life in your home. It's also a space that is not usually cleared on a regular basis. Life is just too busy to regularly keep up with all the contents of the garage. Therefore, you may have things in your garage that have long since ceased being useful to you. However, those things could possibly be useful to someone else. Check out the contents of your garage for things you and your family have outgrown or have decided not to use anymore.

If you have children, there is a strong likelihood that you could have children's toys and/or sporting and recreational equipment that is no longer used. Perhaps your children have moved beyond soccer and baseball and now prefer skateboarding. Are there old tennis rackets that no one uses? Are the days of going to the beach as a family over, because your children are grown and have families of their own?

Does anyone in your home ride a bike anymore? And, if you wanted to ride, are the bikes in your garage the kind you want to ride? Perhaps you have skis and ski equipment there but have given up on finding good snow where you live. Let those things go to make room for items associated with your current interests.

You may have been a gardening enthusiast when your back was more limber, or you had more time for it. If your interest, your physical health, and/or your schedule have changed, making it unlikely that you'll do much gardening, pare down the gardening tools and extra planting pots to reflect your current level of interest and ability to work in your garden.

I often find about three to seven coolers in a family garage. Perhaps they harken back to the days when you once camped or entertained more than you currently do. Can you release a few of them?

Finally, garages tend to accumulate those items that you just had to have because they seemed like just the right thing to meet a specific need or desire. But, some of those items were a big disappointment to you. They didn't work the way you thought they would. Perhaps they make a lot of noise. Or, maybe you couldn't figure out how to make them work properly. Because you spent money on them, you hesitate to just give them away. I think of those things as mistakes; bloopers. We all make purchasing mistakes. If you hold on to those items you are keeping a physical reminder that you made a mistake. They hold "you made a mistake" energy in place. Since like energies attract more of the same, keeping them attracts more mistakes. It's really OK to let them go. Forgive yourself or the company that made them for the disappointment, donate or trash those items, and move on!

Make your garage reflect your current life, your current needs for home improvement and home maintenance equipment, and your current sporting, gardening, and recreational needs. You'll enjoy having more space, and your garage will be up to date!

The Overwhelming Garage: Seven Steps to Get Started

You look at your garage. It's all you can do to resist running straight for the sofa and the remote control. You promised yourself (and perhaps your spouse) that today was the day you'd finally tackle the garage. But,

Garage

how to start when your brain has shut down and you feel overwhelmed by the enormity of the task?

Getting started on an overwhelming clutter clearing/organizing task can be the hardest part of the project (with finishing the task coming in at a close second). Sometimes, it takes sheer determination or the threat of a divorce to motivate you to surmount the rock-hard resistance in your soul. The suggestions in this section are offered to help you catapult over being overwhelmed and get started.

- **Remove the largest items from the garage first;** even things that you intend to keep. Doing so immediately shifts energies and makes it easier to think and make decisions.
- **Look for obvious large trash and remove it.** Trash is easy. It's not something to deliberate about. The larger the trash that's removed, the bigger the energy shifts. Big energy shifts help you see and feel that you're making progress, which will keep you motivated to continue working.
- **Look for large items that you can donate** without deliberation and remove them. Again, their removal will cause large energy shifts.
- **Contain small items in bags or boxes.** Small items have a noisy, distracting energy. When you gather them together in a container, without taking the time to sort through them, you immediately see results in the look and feel of your garage. Your nervous system will feel the benefits of fewer distractions. Do not get seduced into making decisions about those small items. If you do, you'll quit, because it's extremely difficult to see and feel progress when dealing with small items.

- **If the floor is dirty, littered with leaves, trash, dog food, or any other type of small trash, sweep up as much of it as you can.** The dirt, grime, and trash have a very annoying negative energy that can repulse you, shut down your brain, and again have you running for the remote. When you sweep it away, you'll immediately shift energies from negative to positive. That shift, and the instant visual reward of clear space, can be just what you need to get going.
- **Ask a friend or willing family member to work with you.** Any overwhelming challenge can be faced more easily with support and assistance. Two brains and strong backs are far superior to one. Besides, you'll have transformed an onerous task into a social event. Company can also distract you from the effects of the negative energy of the space. Be sure to choose a person with whom you have a good relationship; someone who will not try to take over or belittle you for the condition of your garage or the kinds of things you have in it.
- **If you're stuck and having trouble getting motivated to clear and organize your garage on your own, hire an experienced professional organizer** who can both get you started and work with you until the task is done, often much more quickly than you could ever do it yourself. When you pay someone for assistance, you create a deadline for getting started, and the work will get done!

You can get started. If one approach doesn't work for you, try another. Keep at it until you win the war with your resistance and the negative energy in your garage. Creating a clutter-free and organized garage is a great way to improve the feng shui of your home and help you restore a sense of control in all areas of your life!

Garage Organization: The Power of Categories

After you clear out trash and items that can be donated to charities, you are ready to organize what's left. Begin by sorting the remaining items by general categories that define the function of the garage. Those general categories typically include: yard, home maintenance and repair, home storage, recreation, and kitchen overflow.

Once you've gathered all the items associated with a general category, you can then sort them into more specific sub-categories.

Yard
- Large yard equipment
- Lawn and garden tools
- Lawn and garden products

Home Maintenance
- Power tools
- Manual tools
- Tool boxes
- Hardware
- Paint and painting supplies
- Home repair supplies

Recreation
- Sports equipment
- Camping equipment
- Vacation equipment
- Coolers

Kitchen Overflow
- Serving dishes
- Cooking utensils
- Food items
- Beverages
- Paper products

Once you've grouped items into the specific sub-categories within a general category, you can then create homes by identifying a region of the garage where the general category will be located. For example, all home maintenance/repair supplies and equipment could live on the front wall (immediately in front of cars) of the garage. Yard supplies and tools could be located on a shelf in one corner, recreation equipment stored in another corner, and kitchen overflow items on shelving close to the door into the house.

Locate the regions based on how often you need to use the items in the various categories and where you will use them. There is no right way to locate the regions. A good rule of thumb is to keep categories of items that are used most often in areas where they can be easily accessed and returned once used. For example, it makes good sense to locate kitchen overflow items near the door into the house since you will use them in the house. It's common for the door into the house to be located near the kitchen. A shelf with lawn and garden supplies might be located close

Garage

to the garage door opening because those items will be used outside the garage.

A category of items that is used weekly for much of the year (like yard equipment), needs to be close at hand. Categories that are used once or twice a year, (like beach, camping, and other occasional-use recreational equipment), can be stored in places that are more difficult to access, such as high shelves or storage platforms.

It is not always possible to keep all items within a general category in the same area because of size and space limitations and differences in frequency of use. For example, the lawn mower might be stored at the back of the garage to make room for cars to move in and out, even though it's frequently used. However, the rest of the yard equipment is stored on a shelf close to the garage door opening. Baseballs, bats, soccer balls, golf clubs, and other frequently-used recreational equipment could be stored where they can be easily retrieved for regular use. Occasional-use recreation equipment like camping supplies and skiing equipment is best stored in a place that is less easily accessed. There is no need to have less frequently used items taking up prime real estate.

Organizing your garage by regions will make it much easier to find things. If you want to look at the seeds you ordered earlier in the year, you can go directly to the yard region. If you need a screwdriver, you can go directly to the home maintenance and repair section.

Sort your garage items into general categories and sub-categories, and then assign the general categories to specific regions in your garage. It's a great way to create sanity in what can be an overwhelming space.

From Cluttered to Clear in Just One Year

A Great Greeting Is Good Feng Shui in a Garage

Do you primarily enter your home through the garage? If you do, what greets you as you come through the garage door? Most garages are anything but peaceful and welcoming. In fact, the energy of garages, even those that are organized, at best can be quite noisy and overwhelming. There's just so much stuff! You leave the stress of your busy day and drive home only to be greeted by a space that is stressful. It would make me want to park the car on the street or in the driveway and enter through the front door!

If you actually park in your garage, you can't help but be greeted by that noisy space. What can you do to make the greeting more pleasant? Make the space feel better by shifting the noise and negative energies to positive energies.

Following are some suggestions for organizing your garage so you can do just that:

- **Regularly clear out anything you no longer love or use**—be ruthless!
- **Add closed storage cabinets to store the noisiest items,** the little stuff, behind closed doors.
- **Add shelving and see-through plastic containers** to organize and hold categories of like items together.
- **Finish the garage walls** with sheetrock.
- **Paint the finished walls an uplifting color** like buttery yellow or a favorite hue (not red, black, gray, white, or any pale shade that communicates as white).
- **Finish the floor with a paint** made especially for garage

floors to give the space a cleaner, finished look.
- **Hang prints and posters** of favorite places you've visited, favorite sayings, and special people or subjects.
- **Paint the door into the house a bright color** so it will be a positive, welcoming greeting.
- **Add a colorful wreath or an attractive plaque** with a positive quote on the door, next to the door, or above the door to draw your eyes away from noisy negative energies in the garage. It will lift your spirits before entering your home.
- **Keep your garage organized** and the floor swept and relatively clean at all times.

It is possible to create an awesome greeting in your garage. I'll never forget walking into a client's garage to put something away, and as soon as I crossed the threshold I came to a complete stop. A month or two earlier I had helped that client organize her garage. I knew the garage well, and the space I'd just entered felt completely different. It was so much more pleasant and peaceful. What made the difference?

As I looked around I noticed she and her handyman had done two things that made a world of difference:
1. She'd had the floor painted with a special durable cream-colored paint with little dark specks in it, made especially for utilitarian spaces like garages and basements. The paint added light to a space that had formerly been dark and dreary. It also gave the garage a finished look.
2. Originally, she'd had two heavily loaded sets of shelves on the driver's side of the car and one set of shelves on the passenger side. Now all the shelves were on the passenger

side of the car leaving the driver's side completely clear. What a difference it made not to be surrounded by loaded shelves when getting out of the car! Plus, it was really nice to have all the noisy energies on the shelving confined to just one side of the garage.

What can you do to increase the positive energy in your garage? What can you get rid of? What can you move around to create a quieter, more peaceful space? Remember, the energy in your garage can be welcoming and positive or overwhelming and negative. Either energy will affect your own energy every time you enter your home through the garage.

An organized, colorful, and attractive garage will communicate peace, competence, and control. A packed, disorganized, and dirty garage screams of work to do, overwhelm, and loss of control. Isn't it worth the effort to transform your primary entrance from a dirty, disorganized dump into a calm and pleasant greeting? Doing so will set the stage for you to be your best self every time you enter your home!

The Ultimate in Good Garage Feng Shui

I'll never forget being shown into the room where my BNI (Business Network International) group was having its Christmas party in the home of one of our members. The room seemed to be a large multi-purpose room, but something about it felt strange. As I looked around I realized that I was in a garage! The couple who were hosting the party had put ceramic tile on the floor; had finished the walls with sheetrock, paint, and even decorative trim; and had arranged framed pictures on

Garage

the walls. I'd *never* seen anything like it!

For years I've been encouraging clients and seminar participants to treat their garages as rooms instead of dumps, as I've mentioned previously. Never in my wildest dreams did I imagine a garage could be transformed into a space that felt like a lovely, large, clutter-free recreation room. I'm guessing that the owners of that amazing garage must have found other places for their dirty garage items!

From Cluttered to Clear in Just One Year

Garage Clutter Clearing Plan

As I've said before, the garage is one of the top three most overwhelming storage spaces in the home where clutter accumulates. It ranks right up there with the attic and the basement! I even procrastinated writing this section of this book because clearing out and organizing a garage is an overwhelming task just to *think about*!

Set the Stage for Success

1. **Choose a day when the weather is moderate**—not too hot or too cold.
2. **It is preferable to work on reclaiming your garage when the sun is shining.** You will need the extra energy boost you'll get from seeing blue skies and sunlight.
3. **Set a reasonable goal for the work you'll do.** If clearing and organizing the whole garage in a day is not remotely possible because it is completely packed or a disorganized mess, set a simpler goal. For example, choose a specific time goal, like working for two hours. Or a specific task goal, like removing everything that obviously will be trashed and hauled to the dump. That way you'll will experience success quickly. Your satisfaction in accomplishing a specific goal will set the stage for future successes. Any progress will shift the energies in the space from negative to positive. If you choose to clear your garage in multiple clearing sessions, be sure to set a schedule for subsequent sessions.
4. **Get help from other family members, friends or a professional organizer.** It is much easier to clear out a garage

Garage

when you do it with someone else. You definitely need help if the job is too overwhelming or you need the assistance of others to lift and move various items stored there. Having help will make this project a social event of sorts, and the camaraderie of working with others can distract you from the enormity of the task.

5. **Take a before picture of the garage.** Also take photos along the way to chart your progress. Having a "before" picture will allow you to see where you started and provide you with proof of your progress as you move through the project. An "after" picture will give you cause for great celebration when you're finished.

6. **Plan a reward following your work on the garage.** Choose something that can be the carrot at the end of the stick; something to look forward to when you reach your garage clutter-clearing goal. Consider a lunch out or an adventure with family. Treat yourself to a nap or ice cream. Or, schedule the clearing before a ball game you can enjoy watching when you're done.

Where Not to Start

1. **Don't start with small things.** If you start with small items like nuts, screws, small tools and the like, you will make little progress quickly, and your brain is likely to shut down. You must see significant results immediately to build enough momentum to keep working at what can be a long, overwhelming and exhausting task.

2. **Don't try to decide what goes where.** When a garage is in a chaotic state or is filled to the gills, its negative energy can

be so overwhelming that the planning part of your brain will freeze. It's best if you first create some open space by clearing out items for trash or to donate. Then when the garage contains only those items that are currently useful to you, decide the locations of various categories of items.

Where to Start
Begin with what's easiest and what will create the biggest energy shift.
1. **Remove your car** if you are storing it in the garage.
2. **Remove any large items that you intend to continue to store in the garage,** like lawn tractors, lawn mowers, bicycles, etc. When you move large items out of the garage at least temporarily, you will experience the benefit of a major energy shift. You'll create space that will make it much easier to think clearly so you can make good decisions about your plan of action.
3. **Remove obvious trash** and create a trash/dump area outside the garage door, the bigger the trash items the better. Examples include broken furniture that isn't worth repairing, large cardboard boxes, broken tools, ancient coolers, dry rotted air mattresses, and ancient paint cans.
4. **Remove large items that you no longer use** and create a donation area outside the garage door separate from the trash/dump area. Old beach umbrellas, beach chairs, air mattresses, bicycles, sports equipment, furniture, and old tools that are never used are the types of items that fall into this category.

Garage

Once you've removed enough things to begin to see progress and feel the benefit of energies shifting from negative to positive, it will be easier to begin to systematically review everything in the garage to determine if each item is still something that you are likely to use in the future.

Guidelines for Systematic Review
1. **Start wherever it is easiest to start.**
2. **Focus on the biggest items first.**
3. **Allow yourself to jump around,** as long as you are still making progress.
4. **Move items to be donated or thrown away out of the garage** into designated donation boxes or trash cans as soon as possible. Getting them out of the space will free up energy that will help motivate you to keep going.
5. **As you work, begin clumping items by function**: yard equipment and supplies, sporting equipment, home maintenance and repair, tools, hardware, pet equipment and supplies, cleaning supplies, etc. Don't worry about where the permanent homes will be for the clumps. That is best determined when a majority of the clearing is done.
6. **Ask yourself these questions about each item**: Do I/we use this item? Am I likely to use it in the future? Is it still in good condition? Is it worthy of being kept in the prime real estate of my garage?
7. **If you find it difficult to ask the above questions** because you feel overwhelmed by the disorder in the space, switch to clumping like items so you can get a better idea of how many items you have in each category. Seeing that you have twenty planters when you're only likely to use five in a given

year could motivate you to release some of the planters that are not in pristine condition.

8. **Work from largest items to smallest items** when sorting items by type, clumping like items, and evaluating items.
9. **If you start feeling overwhelmed while working, stop**, take a deep breath and try to figure out what shut you down. Did you gravitate to small items and have difficulty making decisions about them? Did you look at the whole project and think, "I'll never get this done?" Are you feeling put off by the nastiness of the space, the dirt, grime, dust, dead bugs and leaves? Once you've determined what shut you down, make a course correction and continue. For example, if you found yourself sorting small items like nuts and bolts instead of larger items like potting supplies or cleaning supplies, shift from the smaller items to larger items. If your thoughts of not being able to finish the project shut you down, switch your thoughts to something like, "This is hard, but I am getting it done" or "I can get done over time by working in two-hour blocks." If the dust and dirt are really affecting your ability to work in the space, take a few moments to do a quick sweep of the garage to remove the worst of the dirt. Resist the urge to do a true cleaning at this point in the process.

Once you have reviewed all items, removing those that will be donated or trashed, and sorting the remaining items by function, you are ready to create permanent homes for the things that will be housed in the garage.

Garage

Guidelines for Creating Homes for Each Function

1. **Locate functions close to where they will be used.** If you decide to have a kitchen overflow area, to hold occasional use items that don't fit in the kitchen, locate it near the door into the house. Yard supplies and sports equipment can be located closer to the garage door since they will always be used outside the garage.
2. **Don't mix items of different functions.** For example, don't mix light bulbs with fertilizer. One is a household supply and the other a yard supply.
3. **Create clear boundaries between functions.** It's best not to mix items of different functions on the same shelf. For example, use one shelf or set of shelves for all household supplies, another shelf or set of shelves for all yard supplies.
4. **Some items will have to be located in one particular area because of their size. Whenever possible locate other items associated with the same function close by.** For example, lawn mowers and large yard equipment may only fit in the far-right corner of your garage when your car is parked in the garage. In that case, if space allows, locate a shelving unit holding smaller yard equipment and supplies nearby.
5. **It's sometimes impossible to keep all items of a particular function in the same area.** Perhaps there is just one area where bicycles can be located for easy access, but that area has no room for smaller sports equipment.

    In cases like that, you must **create two separate areas for that function**, one for large sports equipment and another for smaller sports equipment. It is recommended, however, that you locate both areas as close together as possible, for

example, on the same side of the garage.
6. **Contain small items within one function in a way that makes those items visible and easy to find.** Good containers include clear plastic bins or drawer units on casters; toolboxes; and organizers that have many little drawers for things like nuts, bolts, and screws.
7. **Take a photo to document your success when everything has a home and you've swept out your garage.** That photo can also serve as a reminder of the location of each function if your garage becomes disorganized again. Knowing where functions belong will make getting reorganized that much easier the next time—if there is a next time.

When you're done with clearing clutter and reclaiming order in your garage, pat yourself on the back for your hard work. Be sure to ask for help from all other family members to help maintain the new order. I recommend that you bring family members into the garage and actually show them where items of each function belong. Seeing the newly cleared and organized space will convey the message that helping to maintain a clutter-free and organized garage is a family responsibility, that maintaining order in the garage is very important to you, and that an organized, clutter-free garage is essential because it reduces stress in your family. If every family member views maintaining an orderly garage as one of their responsibilities, you are less likely to end up facing a garage nightmare again.

Garage order does seem to melt down over time because of time constraints, other obligations, and crisis periods in your life. It's important that you restore order as soon as possible when it does melt down, because the more chaotic the space becomes, the more likely the nega-

Garage

tive energy of the disorder will be experienced as overwhelming, making it that much more difficult to tackle.

Make a commitment to maintain garage order and you'll reap the benefits of lower stress and greater feelings of control in all areas of your life. The garage is a big space. Keep it clutter-free and organized and its condition can anchor great quantities of positive energy in your home and in your life.

From Cluttered to Clear in Just One Year

CHAPTER 12

The Attic

"I like attics. They're as peaceful as God's church. Alone and apart, but a body can hear everything. The past stacked up like forgotten memories, but with a small effort, brought down and enjoyed again."
—Kim Harrison

The Ultimate Challenge: The Attic!

My guess is that clearing out the attic is not one of your favorite activities! However, it probably is a permanent line item on your weekend "To Do" list, way down at the bottom. Most people plan to clear out their attic . . . someday. It's one of the clutter clearing tasks most dreaded by people of all ages. Why is that?

You're probably thinking, "Duh! It's an enormous task! It's an overwhelming task!" And, you're right. Part of the reason attic clutter clearing is one of the top most procrastinated clutter clearing and organizing tasks is because it's hard to do. It is overwhelming. Let's look at some of the factors that make attic clutter clearing so difficult.

- **Most attics are large open spaces** that can hold an enormous number of items; too much space, too much stuff!
- **Most attics don't come with shelving units** and other structures that make it easy to store things in an organized way. Therefore, it's quite common for attics to become and feel chaotic and disorganized.
- **Attics are dusty, dirty places unless they are finished spaces.** Dust and dirt are sources of negative energy that tend to repel you and affect negatively affect your energy.
- **Most attics are not temperature controlled**, therefore in many regions they become ovens from late spring until early fall, and freezers during the winter months. It's not comfortable to work in an attic, unless the weather is mild and even slightly cool. That really limits the window of time during which attic clutter clearing is even possible.
- **Access to many attics involves using stairs**; either the pull-down kind or (if you're lucky) regular stairs. Either way, climbing up and down stairs to haul things out that are to be donated or trashed never ranks high on anyone's list as an enjoyable activity. Climbing up and down stairs requires that you be in fairly good shape and takes a lot of energy!
- **Most attics don't have windows and, therefore, are dark places.** Dark places have low energy; they are places where you don't want to do anything at all, much less make decisions about things that are dusty and dirty. Even with sufficient lighting, they are often grim environments.
- **Most attics are unfinished, utilitarian places.** Places that are not finished and purely utilitarian are usually not carefully tended and maintained. It's far easier to dump things in an

The Attic

attic than in one of the finished living spaces in a home that people other than the family might see.

Is it any wonder that attics are dumped in, neglected, and often ignored? They are valued as a space to store stuff; to put things that aren't currently active so they're out of sight. But, beyond that, they are only occasionally visited, rarely cleared out, rarely cleaned, and seldom organized. No wonder most people groan when they think of their attic!

Attic Clutter Clearing: Get Help

Facing a cluttered attic is *not* a one-person job. Its negative energies and the prospect of many trips up and down stairs will put off even the most conscientious individual. Why set yourself up for procrastination and failure? Get help!

How can getting help make a difference?
- **A date to clear the attic will be scheduled on your calendar,** so it will be harder to procrastinate facing your monster.
- **If you choose a person who really wants to help you, usually not children or husbands,** the time you spend together becomes a social event.
- **You and your helper can more easily move heavy items out of the space.**
- **You and your helper can share the effort of going up and down stairs,** so no one gets completely worn out.
- **You have someone to consult with when making decisions** about what to keep and what to toss.

- **You will likely make two to four times the progress** than you could do on your own.
- **You are less likely to run away from the project** when you reach a point where you're stuck or bored, because you'll have the support of another person to help you move through it.
- **You'll have someone with whom you can celebrate** when you finish the job.

You're probably thinking, "Yeah, who is going to be willing to face my attic horror with me?" Actually, many people enjoy helping someone else with their clutter nightmare. It's far easier to help someone else than to deal with your own clutter. Don't assume that all requests for help will be met with a negative response. Some people really do get pleasure from helping people they care about.

There are several options for finding help with your attic clutter clearing project:
- **Trade clutter clearing time with a friend** who would also benefit from having support to get their clutter clearing done.
- **Find a high school or college student** who would enjoy earning some spending money by helping you clear out your attic.
- **Hire a professional organizer** who is trained to tackle a large project like an attic.

As a last resort, ask family members to block off time to help you clear your attic. I offer this as a last resort because you're likely to get more push back from family members. Plus, it's more difficult to get a specific time commitment from them. You are also more likely to run into power struggles with family members. Clearing an attic is hard enough to contemplate and do without the added challenge of conflict and power struggles. Ideally, getting help should make facing and completing the task a more pleasurable experience. Trying to get the job done with family members could make an already overwhelming task seem monumental.

Find the right help and get your attic clutter clearing done!

What Does Not Belong in Your Attic?

Sometimes it's hard to know where to start when you're tackling attic clutter clearing. One way to eat that elephant is to look for things that really should not be stored in the attic, either because they deteriorate in the temperature extremes or because they will never be accessed there.

Here are some items that I find in attics that would best be stored elsewhere:
- **Candles and any type of item that melts.** Attics in the summer are ovens, definitely not the place for things that become soft in high temperatures.
- **Framed art.** Attics are dirty places, and the temperature extremes damage most prints and paintings.
- **Photographs.** Photographs tend to deteriorate over time. Put them in the attic and you'll speed up that process exponentially.
- **Books.** The only reason to hold onto books is to be able to read them. Books in the attic can't be accessed to read,

and the temperature extremes will make the pages become brittle and deteriorate. If they get covered in attic dust and dirt, their negative energy will make them very unappealing to read.
- **Sporting equipment.** If sporting equipment is to be used with any regularity, it should be stored in a garage, shed, or utility room for easy access. You are less likely to use sporting equipment if it's hard to access.
- **Memorabilia.** If those papers, cards, and other mementos are so precious, why are you torching them in summer and freezing them in winter? Also, how can you share them with anyone when they are so difficult to access? The temperature extremes in the attic will transform precious papers into fire starter material.

Clearing out the above items is a great way to get started with attic clutter clearing. Once those items are moved out, you'll have shifted some energy from negative to positive, freed some energy that is then available to you. You will also have gained more space to work on items that *are* best stored in an attic.

Love Your Attic

I can imagine that many of you are thinking, "Love my attic. Are you kidding?" What would it take for you to love your attic? Attics are not places that we think about loving. They are storage spaces, not areas where you hang out. But, imagine going into your attic without a sense of dread. Imagine actually looking forward to entering your attic. What

The Attic

would that attic look like? How would it feel?

The following factors can contribute to having an attic that you love:
- It has been cleared of all things that you no longer love or use and gets cleared at least once a year.
- A majority of the items stored there are accessed at least once a year.
- It is well organized, so you can find things easily.
- It has space to move around.
- The floors have been swept or vacuumed to remove dust and grime.
- The things you use most often are conveniently located for easy access.
- Everything in the space is in good condition and in good working order.
- Everything in the space has a purpose.
- It has good lighting.

An attic like the one I'm describing would certainly not feel like the burden that most attics seem to be. It would still be a storage area, not a place to spend time, but I'll bet you'd be less likely to procrastinate going there. Perhaps that's as close to loving your attic as you'll get.

Why Keep an Attic Clean?

Attics are storage areas. As such, most people lower their standards for cleanliness in that type of utilitarian space. After all, attics "out of sight, out of mind." They aren't a public space that people other than family and close friends are likely to see. So, why bother to sweep up dust, dirt, and grime? Why pick up trash?

Dust, dirt, grime, and trash hold very negative energies. Just think back to your response to a very dirty space you recently accessed, perhaps a garage, a dirty refrigerator, or a space that's been neglected for some time. Most people have an instinctual urge to retreat from those types of spaces. Why? Because they have a predominance of negative energy. We are drawn to spaces with peaceful, positive energies. We are repulsed by spaces that are predominated by negative energies. Even the positive energies of lovely things in a dirty space are not enough to make us want to spend time there. The dirtier the space, the more likely you'll continue to avoid it, neglect it, and dump in it, compounding the dirt and grime.

Check it out! Notice how you feel and what you do in dirty spaces.

Haul your vacuum cleaner to your attic and suck up the dust, dirt, and grime. Pick up the trash. Then step back and take a moment to feel the burst of positive energy you've released by eliminating sources of toxic, negative energy. It could be the first step to a more positive relationship with your attic!

The Right Stuff for Good Feng Shui in Your Attic

Feng shui teaches that items that are static, not moving, take on a negative energy over time. It's quite common to take things to the attic when you aren't quite ready to part with them, when you don't know what else to do with them, when you want things out of your living space, or when

The Attic

you don't want to make a decision about what to do with them. What typically ends up in the attic is a wide assortment of things, some that get used at least once a year and some that take up permanent residence there. Lots of static stuff!

As the highest room in the house, your attic holds the energy of your hopes and aspirations. Given that attics are storage areas where items don't tend to move very often, your attic is also quite possibly a haven of negative energies that could be having a negative effect on achieving your hopes and aspirations.

One way to make sure your attic has the best energy possible is to make sure that the majority of its contents are things that get used at least once a year.

The following are categories that fit that description:
- Luggage
- Seasonal decorations
- Off-season clothing
- Camping equipment
- Occasional-use kitchen items
- Party items

No doubt there will be categories of items stored in your attic that are rarely accessed, like archived financial and legal documents. However, if you keep those more static categories to a minimum and maintain order and cleanliness in your attic, its energy will be more positive than negative. It will no longer be a haven of negative energy, and you will likely find it easier to achieve your hopes and aspirations. Perhaps for the first time ever you'll be able to identify what your hopes and aspirations are! Clearing clutter and keeping the energies in your attic alive and positive are also great ways to improve mental clarity!

When the energy of your attic is improved, so too will be the energy of your entire home. Good energy equates to a good life. Isn't it worth it to make your attic a home for items that are alive with positive energy instead of leaving it as a static dump of items with negative energy?

A New Vision for Your Attic

Yes, it's possible to maintain a relatively clutter-free attic. However, it's not likely to happen unless you commit to making that happen and make sure all family members make the same commitment. It won't happen because of your desire alone.

In my experience, many attics over time become dumping grounds precisely because no thought and planning goes into creating something other than a dumping ground. They seem to become the step-children to the "real" rooms of the house; those you live in and that other people might see. Attics are "out of sight, out of mind."

The first important step to maintaining a clutter-free attic is to think about it differently. Instead of viewing it as an easy place to stash things you don't want to deal with in the moment, consider it a place to store your valuables until you next use them. Valuables are things you or family members are likely to use in the future. If only valuables are permitted in your attic, you'll be less likely to dump things that are not really valuable.

The attic is the place in your house that holds the energy of your hopes and aspirations. Keep that knowledge "top of mind." Use it to remind you that what you put in your attic will either support your hopes and aspirations or block them. For example, a new bedspread purchased

The Attic

and stored in the attic until you've finished painting your bedroom holds the positive energy of anticipation and positive change in your living space and your life. Worn out carpets and old bedspreads that you couldn't part with and will probably never use again hold negative energies that will block hopes and aspirations.

Change your thoughts about your attic's purpose and importance, and you'll motivate yourself to intentionally make good decisions about what gets stored there. You'll treat your attic with more respect. Valuables that hold the energy of your hopes and aspirations deserve the time and attention it takes to keep them accessible and organized.

From Cluttered to Clear in Just One Year

Attic Clutter Clearing Plan

Your attic. It's supposed to be a great storage area in your home, and at first, it probably was. But over time most attics become dirty places cluttered with all kinds of stuff, much of which is not all that valuable. But, going up there and doing something about it? If you're like most people, you put off clearing out and organizing your attic until the cows come home!

As with the garage, I again procrastinated writing this plan. Like garages, attics are complicated places to clear and organize. So much stuff. So many kinds of things. Lots of negative energies from dust, dirt, grime, and deteriorating static stuff. No wonder people spend more time thinking they should clear their attics than actually doing the work!

As noted earlier in this chapter, the attic is the area of your home that holds the energies of your hopes and aspirations. When it is packed, disorganized, and dirty, there are many energies that block achieving your hopes and aspirations. Use that knowledge to fuel your determination to create a clutter-free and organized attic.

Set the Stage for Success
1. **Choose the right time of year.** If you live in an area with four seasons, the best times for tackling an attic are usually early spring and fall. Since most attics are not temperature controlled, make sure you do it at a time when the attic is neither too hot nor too cold. It's important that you feel comfortable working in your attic; otherwise you will avoid doing it, and if you get started, you'll have the perfect excuse to quit.

The Attic

2. **Choose the right time of day.** Choose the time of day when the attic temperature will be comfortable and, equally important, when your mental energy will be high. I prefer mornings before the roof has had time to heat up. I am also a "morning person," so it's easier for me to make decisions in the morning.
3. **Schedule a date or dates to clear your attic.** Treat it as you would a dentist or doctor's appointment; a firm commitment that you will keep.
4. **Set a reasonable goal for what you'll accomplish.** Some attics are small and can be completed in one clearing session of two to eight hours. Others require multiple sessions because they are large and/or contain huge quantities of items accumulated over decades. If clearing and organizing the whole attic in a day is not remotely possible because it is completely packed, choose a specific time goal, like working for one hour, or a specific task goal, like clearing one side, or removing specific items that can be donated or hauled to the dump. That way you will set yourself up for success. You'll accomplish that specific goal, and feel good about that accomplishment which will set the stage for future successes. Any progress will shift the energies in the space from negative to positive. If you choose to clear your attic in multiple clearing sessions, be sure to set a schedule for subsequent sessions.
5. **Get help from at least one other person, preferably someone who is in good shape and relatively strong.** Most attics are accessed by stairs. Clearing attics usually requires multiple trips up and down stairs, as well as lifting

and hauling items that can be bulky and/or heavy. That is definitely one of the barriers to getting the work done! Trying to make decisions about what to keep, what to get rid of, and how to organize the space in addition to doing all the hauling of items to be trashed or donated all alone is a setup for failure. Find someone . . . a helpful friend, a willing family member, a teenager or college student who would like to earn a little money . . . to assist you with the leg work. It can make all the difference in how quickly the work progresses or whether you tackle the job at all.
6. **Be sure you have adequate lighting in the space.** Light is energy; energy that will make decision-making much easier. It's very difficult to make decisions in a dim space. Bring in extra lighting if you need to.
7. **Plan a reward after each clearing session.** It's helpful to have something to look forward to after you face a difficult task like clearing your attic, something you'll only allow yourself if you make progress in your attic.

Remember, getting started in your attic is a significant hurdle to surmount. The negative energies in an attic created by dirt, dust, grime, and all that static stuff can cause incredible resistance in even the most conscientious homeowner. Just remember, once you get started and begin to see progress, you'll probably find yourself feeling relieved to be dismantling your most dreaded clutter-clearing nightmare. In addition, your energy and enthusiasm are likely to increase once you can see and feel progress being made.

The Attic

Where Not to Start
1. **Don't start with small things.** If you start with small items like loose toys, books, and paper, you will make little progress quickly and your brain is likely to shut down. You must see significant results immediately to build enough momentum to keep working at this big job.
2. **Don't start by trying to decide where to store specific items.** You will want to create a new order once your attic is clear and it is easy to see its contents. However, when it is in a chaotic state or is filled to the gills, your attic's negative energy can be so overwhelming that the planning part of your brain will freeze. It's best if you first do a significant amount of clearing and create some open space before you try to decide the permanent locations of various categories of items.

Where to Start
As with the garage, begin this project with what's easiest and what will create the biggest energy shifts.
1. **Take a picture of the attic.** Having a "before" picture will allow you to see your progress as you move through the project, and you'll be thrilled to compare it to the "after" picture you take upon completion!
2. **Identify a donation area and a separate trash area somewhere on the floor below the attic,** in places that are easy to get to once you descend the stairs. That way you can take items you decide to part with to those locations and they will already be sorted when you are ready to them to the trash or to your vehicle for transportation to a charity.

3. **Remove *large* items that you can donate or throw away first.** Those items will be things you no longer love or use, things that you know will no longer serve you in the life you have or want to have. Move large items first so you can immediately see and feel progress.
4. **Gather up and remove any obvious loose trash into bags or boxes and remove them immediately.** Trash is a source of negative energy. It is irritating. Remove it immediately to make the space look and feel better. That shift will encourage you and make continuing so much easier.
5. **Remove items that don't belong in the attic** because they could be harmed by temperature extremes, or because they are frequently used and the attic is not the most convenient location for easy access. This could include candles or any type of item that melts, framed art, photographs, books, sporting equipment, or memorabilia. Once you've removed enough things to begin to see progress and feel the benefit of the energy shifts, it will be easier to begin to systematically review everything in the attic to determine if each item is still something that you are likely to use in the future.

Guidelines for Systematic Review
1. **Identify the major categories of items that will be housed in your attic.** Make sure those categories are things that have a high probability of being used at least once a year. Using things activates their energies and keeps them positive. Regularly accessed items include luggage, seasonal decorations, off-season clothing, camping equipment, or occasional-use kitchen and party items. Items that are less

regularly used that may have to be housed in the attic are archived papers and furniture being stored for use in the future.
2. **Start wherever it is easiest to start,** particularly in areas where you know you are likely to find many things that can be donated or trashed.
3. **Focus on the biggest items first.**
4. **Allow yourself to jump around** as long as you are getting rid of things and are still making progress.
5. **Make frequent trips to move items to be donated or thrown away out of the attic** to the donation and trash areas on the floor below. Getting them out of the space will free up energy that will help keep you motivated to keep going. Be sure to return to the attic as soon as you've dropped off those items.
6. **As you work, begin clumping items by category**: luggage, off-season clothing, seasonal decorations, occasional-use kitchen items, storage bins, etc. Don't worry about where the permanent homes will be for those clumps. That is best determined when a majority of the clearing is done.
7. **Ask yourself these questions about each item:** Do I/we use this item? Am I likely to use it in the future? Is it still in good condition? Is it worthy of being kept in the area of my hopes and aspirations? Does it in any way hold the energy of my hopes and aspirations? For example, luggage holds the energy of travel and fun trips in the future. Seasonal decorations hold the energy of future celebrations and shared times with family and friends.
8. **If you find it difficult to ask the above questions because**

you feel overwhelmed by the disorder in the space, look for more things that be donated or trashed. Or, switch to clumping like items so you can get a better idea of how many items you have in each category. Seeing that you have five pieces of luggage the same size when you're only likely to use one or two on a regular basis could motivate you to release some of the suitcases that are not in pristine condition.

9. **Work from largest items to smallest items** when sorting items by type, clumping like items, and evaluating items.

10. **If you start feeling overwhelmed while working, stop, take a deep breath and try to figure out what shut you down.** Did you gravitate to small items and have difficulty making decisions about them? Did you look at the whole project and think, "I'll never get this done?" Are you feeling put off by the nastiness of the space, the dirt, grime, and dust? Once you've determined what shut you down, make a course correction and continue. For example, if you found yourself trying to make decisions about a box of old papers, shift from the paper to larger items. If your thoughts of not being able to finish the project shut you down, switch your thoughts to something like, "This is hard, but I am getting it done." If the dust and dirt are really affecting your ability to work in the space, take a few moments to vacuum the floors that are visible. Just removing that dirt can give you an energy boost.

11. **Some categories of items are best sorted and evaluated elsewhere.** If you find it difficult to evaluate boxes of small items and papers, haul them down to the lower level to be evaluated in a space that has more light and better energies.

The Attic

Once you have reviewed all items, removed those that will be donated or trashed, and sorted items by function, you are ready to create permanent homes for the various categories that will be housed in the attic.

Guidelines for Creating Homes for Each Category

1. **Locate things close to where they will be used.** For example, your luggage would best be located close to the attic opening, since luggage gets used more often during the year than other attic items.

    Furniture that is being held for children going to college in a number of years could be stored further from the attic opening, because it will not be used until it is removed from the attic.

2. **Don't mix items of different categories.** For example, don't mix seasonal decorations with luggage. Mixing items of different categories makes seeing and finding any one thing much more difficult. It's much easier to find things if all items of the same type are located together in one location and not mixed with other types of things.

3. **Create clear boundaries between categories.** For example, if you have shelves in your attic, use one shelf or set of shelves for all off-season clothing and another shelf or set of shelves for all archived taxes and other paperwork. Also, it's best not to mix items of different categories on the same shelf, if possible.

4. **Be sure to put small items within any category in clear plastic bins, so they will be visible and won't get lost among larger items.** Always use clear plastic bins for storage. That

way you won't have to label the bins because their contents is visible.

5. **Once your attic has been cleared and organized by category, vacuum the floors to remove all dust and dirt.** Then enjoy the luscious feeling of a clutter-free, organized, and clean attic!
6. **Finish by taking a photo to document your success.** That photo can also serve as a reminder of the location of each category when your attic becomes disorganized again.

When you're done with clearing clutter and reclaiming order in your attic, pat yourself on the back for your hard work. Be sure to ask for help from all other family members to maintain the new order. Bring family members into the attic and show them where items of each category belong. Establish a No Dumping Policy for your attic, and ask all family members to honor it. Consider putting a NO DUMPING sign on your attic door (at least initially) to remind everyone of your new commitment to treat your attic differently than it was treated in the past.

Beware that attic order does seem to melt down over time, because of time constraints, temperature challenges (like extreme heat and cold, which make it uncomfortable to put things away in their proper locations in summer and winter), and crisis periods in your life. Don't despair. It will be easier to reorganize because of the initial order you created. Just make sure you restore order sooner rather than later, before the initial order disappears. The more chaotic the space becomes, the more likely the negative energies of the space will be experienced as overwhelming, making it that much harder to tackle.

Make a commitment to maintain attic order and you'll reap the benefits of lower stress and greater feelings of control in all areas of your life.

The Attic

Keep it clutter-free and organized, and its condition can anchor great quantities of positive energy in your home and in your life. When the energies of your attic are predominantly positive, you are more likely to attain your hopes and aspirations.

From Cluttered to Clear in Just One Year

CHAPTER 13

Closets

"Opening your closet should be like arriving at a really good party where everyone you see is someone you like."
—Amy Fine Collins

The Closet Decluttering Debate: Pull Everything Out or Not?

When tackling a closet clutter clearing project, is it best to pull everything out and completely empty a closet, or is it best to leave things in the closet and just pull out the things that can go elsewhere?

Rarely do I recommend completely emptying a closet. Why is that? Closets typically hold huge quantities of things. It takes time to empty a closet and put clothes back after decisions are made about what to keep or donate. That time would be better spent looking for items to give away. Plus, the sheer volume of things coming out of a closet can overwhelm most people and shut down the clutter clearing process.

Plus, people are often overly optimistic about how long it will take to clear a closet. If there is an error in time estimation, it is a much easier task to clean up and close the closet door until the next clearing session if things remain inside and are sorted there, instead of having all of the closet contents spread around the room.

There are usually some things in every closet that will remain just where they are, even after you've sorted and evaluated all of the contents. Moving them out is unnecessary work.

Items that will remain in the closet in approximately the same location provide a kind of structure for you to use as a guide when sorting and placing things back in the closet.

It is usually possible to clear clutter from a closet without emptying the whole closet. The only reasons for totally emptying a closet are: to give it a completely new function; you're packing to move; you're having a new closet system installed; you want to paint the inside of the closet; or you're changing the closet flooring.

Instead of totally emptying a closet, I recommend that first you pull out only those things that are scattered all over the floor. Doing that will immediately calm some of the chaotic energy in the closet.

Work with the rest of the items in the closet from their locations, unless it becomes apparent that dealing with all of them inside the closet is difficult. For many items you'll be able to make decisions about whether to keep them, get rid of them, or change their location from inside the closet.

Feeling overwhelmed? If you find yourself feeling overwhelmed, confused, or frustrated while evaluating things inside the closet, take that as a sign that you should pull them out and make decisions about them outside the closet. For example, you may find you need to remove some items because they are getting in your way, or sorting things into categories cannot be easily done within the closet. In those cases, remove just those items and deal them outside the closet.

Take out only those items that cannot be easily evaluated and organized from within the closet. Remember, you don't want to make more work for yourself by pulling out more items than necessary. And, you don't want to leave your clutter clearing session with the closet and surrounding area messier than when you started.

Your Personal Closet Is a Reflection of You!

Your personal closet is the most important closet in the house. Well, from a feng shui perspective it is, anyway! Your closet is an outward extension of you, and your clothes hold your energy. Take a look at your closet. How are you doing right now? Are you calm, spacious, and organized? Or, are you a chaotic jumble of stuff?

How can I be so certain of the significance of your closet? For thirteen years I've helped clients clear and organize their closets, assisting them to make decisions about what to keep and what to toss using the "Love It, Use It, or Lose It" method of clutter clearing mentioned in the first chapter. Clothing items that a client still loves and/or uses are kept, because they have the best energy. Those that are not loved or used at least once a year are tossed or donated. By going through that process over and over again with clients, it has become apparent to me that clothing holds important associations with the different aspects of their owner's lives, some of which are current and some of which are outdated.

During the clearing process, clients have the chance to "get current" about who they are by identifying those clothes they still love, that still fit, that make them look attractive, that are comfortable, and that are useful given the owner's current activities. In the process, clients let go of volumes of clothing that are too small, that are suited only to a former occupation, that feel uncomfortable, that fit poorly, that are of poor quality, that hold negative associations, and that are permanently stained.

When we finish our clearing sessions, each client has more clarity about their current self: their current values and lifestyle as well as their preferences in terms of comfort, color, and styles. Clients go from feeling overwhelmed and scattered to feeling clear and empowered within the space of two hours!

Go into your closet and set your intention to create a space that is an accurate reflection of who you are today. With each clothing item ask yourself, "Does this item accurately reflect who I am today? Does it reflect who I want to be today?" If the answer to either question is "no," then let it go! Get clear. Get current. And, get empowered!

Do You Have a Closet from Hell?

When you start cursing you know your closet is really bad! Let me tell you about a closet organizing experience that will hopefully shed some new light on your challenging project!

I was working in the bathroom. My client's closet was so poorly designed because:
1. **The four shelves were set about 6" back inside** an opening that was raised about 18" off the floor.
2. **The opening was narrow,** smaller than the closet width.
3. **The shelves were about 24" deep,** which made reaching

Closets

the back of the top two shelves possible only if I shoved my shoulders through the opening, grabbed hold of the shelves, and fully extended my arm.

That's when I began to experience spontaneous grumbling! **The space was designed in a way that made it a total organizing nightmare!**

What were the designers thinking?!! What happens in a poorly designed closet like this? The homeowner did the best she could, trying to use space that was both inaccessible and inconvenient. However, because the closet was so hard to access, the semblance of order that she tried to establish had clearly melted down to one of those "just shove it in there" spaces.

Though I was sorely tempted to pull out a sledge hammer and widen the opening, I restrained myself and was worked to set up a system within the closet that could work better than the willy-nilly approach that had been tried.

Here's what I did, step-by-step:
- **I started with the big stuff,** pulling all the big things off the floor at the bottom of the closet. I discovered that the bathmats, shower mats, and scatter rugs were all in good shape, so I returned them to the floor of the closet. They were joined by a large medical supply bag, a heating pad, and a hair dryer; large items that would "eat" space if located on upper shelves.
- **I then pulled out all of the sheets and towels** and initially set them aside until I could clear an entire shelf for them. I planned to devote one shelf (second from the top) to them, because it's always a good idea to avoid mixing linens with

other things like toiletries, medicines, etc. As mentioned in the bathroom chapter, large items like sheets and towels could be located higher up in a closet than small items like toiletries because they are easier to see and they are less likely to get lost on the invisible back section of the shelf.

- **I cleared off the first (top) shelf** that had been holding bottles of supplements and old medications. Many of those items had been invisible from outside the closet. They were temporarily placed on the floor for further review of expiration dates later in the process.
- **In reviewing the items on the second, third, and fourth shelves**, I discovered a large collection of scented candles, incense, and air fresheners — "smelly stuff." They were just the type of occasional-use items that, clumped together in box or bin, could be stored on the highest shelf. Since the top shelf was so high that it was almost inaccessible, I knew I needed to find something to put there that would only get accessed occasionally, something that was big enough to be visible from outside the closet. The "smelly stuff" items were perfect for that location.
- **Because the shelves at waist level** (3rd and 4th shelves) were what I call "prime real estate" (the most easily accessible and most visible), I planned to organize the smallest items on those shelves: shampoo and lotion bottles, cleansers, supplements, over-the-counter medications, nail polish and manicure supplies, etc.
- **When I had removed everything from the first, second, third, and fourth shelves** I asked my client to review everything and make decisions about what to toss and what

to keep. I reviewed all the expiration dates of the supplements and over the counter medications and threw away all that were out of date.
- **The remaining "smelly stuff" and linens** were placed on the first and second shelves.
- **I organized larger items on the third and fourth shelves** (bottle of lotions, shampoos, etc. Then we searched for and found containers to house categories of small items that would be stored on the third and fourth shelves.
- **My client found a clear plastic drawer that fit perfectly on one of the shelves.** Since there were a significant number of small items related to manicures and pedicures, I decided to devote the whole container exclusively to nail tools, supplies, and polishes once my client reduced their volume to those that were still useful. Within that container items were separated by type and held in small open containers. I placed the nail supply container on the fourth shelf, because it was the only shelf low enough for the contents of the drawer to be visible when opened.
- **The nail supply container took up about 2/3 of the fourth shelf**, leaving a small space beside it where I located the cleaning supplies. I also found a plastic tray that fit nicely on top of the nail supply container. It became the location for extra razors and razor refills. Putting the tray there kept those small supplies visible and contained, and prevented them from drifting to the back of the closet.
- **Miscellaneous occasional-use items, like back massagers and extra hair brushes**, were located at the back of the third and fourth shelves and positioned so they would be visible

behind the more frequently used items at the front. If items at the front of the shelves get moved and obscure sight of the things at the back, it's not likely to be a big inconvenience, because the latter are only occasional-use items.
- **I suggested to my client that she ask her carpenter to explore whether the opening to the closet could be widened** to create better access to the shelves.

As is probably very apparent from the description above, putting together a closet that allows for visibility and accessibility of most items is like putting together a puzzle. When you add poor closet design to that challenge, creating a functional closet in which order can be maintained over time can seem almost impossible. I like a challenge, but most people would not take the time to solve the puzzle. They'd just limp along, as my client had been doing for years, with a barely functional closet.

If you have a "closet from hell," one that has you stumped, consider hiring a professional organizer to create the initial order. Then it will be your job to maintain that order over time.

Specialized Closet Design: Is It Worth the Cost?

Should you pay the big bucks for a closet designed to your needs? Is it worth the cost? Is it worth the effort it will take to empty the closet and put everything back?

I've worked with a number of clients who bit the bullet and hired a company to do a custom design and installation of their personal closet or their children's closets. Without exception, the custom closet arrangement was far superior to what had existed before.

Closets

Following are some of the benefits my clients experienced:
- There was more usable storage space.
- **There was more structure within the "black hole" of the closet**, so fewer items tended to float without a home and get lost.
- **The process of emptying and refilling their closet** provided two clearing opportunities, when the clothes, shoes, etc. came out and when they went back in.
- **The energy of the new closet felt really good** and motivated clients to respect the space by keeping it neat and organized.
- **Custom closets are considered an asset** when you sell your home.

That being said, I do have a few words of caution to share:
- **Make sure you use a company with a good reputation.** Not all companies produce and stand behind their products. Ask for references for any company you are considering, or go with a company recommended by discerning friends or a professional organizer.
- **Make sure you have a good closet designer.** Designers are not equally skilled. I learned that lesson when I had the opportunity to review the plans of two different designers from two different companies for a client. The difference between the quality of the two designs was startling.
- **For your personal closet, consider working with a same sex designer** because they're likely to have a better grasp of the complexities of your storage needs.
- **Make sure the company has some kind of guarantee for satisfaction.** It is quite common to think that a design is

perfect until you begin putting clothing back into it. It's not uncommon to need to make adjustments to the original design.

Should you get custom designed closets? When your budget allows, I highly recommend it. If you can only do one at a time, start with your personal closet. It has the most effect on your day-to-day functioning, and having that area functioning well will ground you and reduce your stress.

How to Create a Closet with Good Energy

A closet is just a storage place, right? No need to worry about enhancing it! Wrong! As feng shui teaches, everything is connected, therefore the energy of every space in your home or office affects what happens in your life, So, negative energy in a closet is not a good thing! Besides, when you have a closet with awesome energy, you'll take better care of it. You'll enjoy using it. The more you enjoy your closest, the more functional it is likely to be.

How do you enhance a closet? Try this!
- **Paint the walls a color.** White walls in a closet tend to get dingy and look dirty quickly. If there is color on the walls of the room where the closet is located (something other than white or any pale shade that communicates as white), paint the closet the same color as the room. Or, have some fun and paint the closet walls one of your favorite colors that you don't have the nerve to use for a complete room.

- **Add art to your closet.** Yes, art! Often there is a bare wall directly in front of you when you enter the closet. Put a framed photograph or print in that location, preferably something that makes you smile. I have a small quilt hanging in my closet, one that I love but that no longer goes with the decor of my home office.
- **Make sure you have good lighting.** Light is energy. Dim bulbs in closets set up the closet to be a dumping ground. Dim lighting = low energy which will affect your energy and motivation to maintain order in your closet.
- **If you have a dresser or shelving in your closet, display some of your jewelry there.** Ring and necklace holders can be used to display special pieces of jewelry. Their positive energy will affect the overall energy of the closet.

Make your closet a place you love and feel proud of, instead of a dumping ground, and you'll find yourself much more willing to spend time to keep it neat, organized, and up to date!

Six Common Issues That Hinder Maintaining Organized Closets

Failing to keep your closets organized might not be entirely your fault. Here are six of the most common reasons people have problems with maintaining organized closets:

1. **The closet is not set up for successful maintenance.** Setting up a closet for successful maintenance of order means taking the time to create an initial order by using containers and

other organizing products that make access to the items easy. Too often in the rush of a busy life, a closet is just thrown together with good intentions of returning to it at a later date to make improvements. But, that day never comes.

2. **The closet is used by more than one family member.** Any time an area is used by more than one person, the chances of its order melting down increase. It's unlikely that all family members will have the same level of commitment to maintaining an organized space. Often the person who initially established the order just assumes that others will see the order that has been created and help to maintain it. That often isn't the case.

3. **Family members have no idea how to organize and maintain order in a closet.** Closet organizing skills are not taught in schools. Many left-brained folks intuitively know how to organize closets because they are wired for creating structure and organizing anything. People who are right-brain dominant and those who have ADHD, however, are not so lucky. Their wiring often leaves them clueless about how to organize something as complex and daunting as a closet.

Unfortunately, when they don't know how to deal with closet organization, their default is either to do the "throw things in willy-nilly and slam the door" approach or to not bother using the closet at all, leaving volumes of their belongings outside the closet.

4. **Family members are not committed to keeping things organized.** Getting a closet organized and keeping it organized are two very different processes. The first is

Closets

time-limited and often can be completed in one-time period. Keeping a closet organized first requires that family members be conscious of the need to maintain order in the space. Then, they must be willing to make the time (often less than a minute or two) and take the necessary actions to keep it organized despite any personal inconvenience. Too often the importance of helping to keep closets organized doesn't even make it onto the list of responsibilities of all family members.

- **By the way, don't assume that others know that they are responsible for helping to keep closets organized**, that they know how to keep a closet organized, or that they can easily decipher the system you've set up. That's a surefire way to guarantee that people will go about their merry way, looking out for their immediate needs for expediency, and have your closet organization will melt down rapidly. You'll then start feeling resentful because family members aren't doing their part to help keep the closet organized. It's important to show family members how the closets they use are organized and request their help to keep it organized.

5. **The closet is poorly designed.** The most common problem with closet design is having shelves that are too deep. Deep shelves make it impossible to see what's at the back of the closet. Unless items at the back of a deep shelf are large enough to loom over the items at the front of the shelf, they disappear from view and then become the source of negative, dead energies.

- **Another common design problem is having a shelf located underneath hanging clothes.** Items on that shelf become invisible when clothes hang over them. I recommend that nothing be stored on those shelves to avoid losing things under the clothes or being irritated by the clothes every time you retrieve or put away things located there.

- **Most traditional clothes closets have one bar with a single shelf above it.** That design is often too simple to meet the varied needs for storage in homes today. Invariably there is wasted space below short items, and the shelf above becomes a jumble of mixed items like shoes, sweaters, photo albums, memorabilia, and gifts because it is harder to access and maintain order. Custom closet design can transform that type of closet into a highly organized space for maximum storage; one that is less likely to lose its order.

6. **The closet's size is too small for current needs.** Older houses often have small closets, or no closets at all. At the time those houses were built, people had less stuff, and many people stored their clothes in a wardrobe. As our world changed after WWII, many people began to enjoy more affluence and acquire things associated with a "good life." Only then did things that had been viewed as luxuries by past generations become necessities, or at least common-place. Combine small or non-existent closets with the depression-era mindset to "waste not, want not" (and its corresponding imperative to keep anything that is still useful), and you've got the perfect recipe for packed closets.

Closets

Now what? Here are some suggestions:

- **Make time to carefully set up each closet** for optimal functioning.
- **Take the extra seconds required to put things away properly in closets**, rather than shoving them in and closing the door.
- **If the inside of a closet has become messy**, restore order to the closet before it becomes completely disorganized.
- **Create new order in a closet when its function changes**; for example, when new categories of items will be stored there.
- **Live within your closets**. It may require that you purge more and keep less. When closet space is truly inadequate, add pieces of furniture to augment closet storage, like additional dressers, wardrobes and armoires.
- **Educate all family members about how to organize closets and keep them organized**. You may need to give explicit instructions like, "please hang up your coat, put your gloves in this container, return nail polish to this container, etc.," until maintenance behaviors become automatic.
- **Educate everyone in the family about the importance of keeping closets organized**, and make it clear that all family members have responsibility for helping to maintain order in closets they access.
- **If you have the financial means, hire a custom closet company to assess, design, and install custom closets** that meet your specific needs within each closet. Custom closets are easier to keep organized and will add to the resale value of your home.

Closet Clutter-Clearing Plan

It's challenging to write one plan for all closets, given that there are so many different types of closets: bedroom closets, bathroom closets, linen closets, hall closets, coat closets, under the eaves closets, walk-in closets, etc.

So, know that you likely will need to modify the following steps to fit whatever closet you are clearing:

1. **Take a picture of the closet you are tackling.** When you look at it, what thoughts pop into your head? Those thoughts will give you an indication of the energy of the space. Most closets that need clearing have "Help! Too much stuff in here!" energy or "What a mess!" energy. Just notice those thoughts. Don't let them stop you in your tracks. It's just the energy talking. Tell yourself that clearing out this closet is just a problem to be solved and that, once you've completed this task, you will feel lighter and you'll have silenced those nasty conversations.

2. **If possible, be sure you're clear about the function of the closet.** In some cases, the function will be very apparent. A linen closet is a linen closet. A coat closet is a coat closet. But, you may decide you want your walk-in personal closet to also house gifts and gift wrap, since you need a home for those things and the closet is so spacious. In some cases, you won't know all the closet functions until you clear and sort the contents. But, whenever possible, if a closet is going to serve more than one function, you'll want to identify those

Closets

functions and plan for accommodating them as you work. As with multi-purpose rooms, a multi-purpose closet is more challenging to organize and keep organized. That also means that clearing out that type of closet can be a time-consuming, complicated process.

3. **Remove only those items that impede your ability to work within the closet, to see and maneuver things.** If, for example, the floor is a chaotic mess, remove all items on the floor. By doing that you'll immediately calm down the energies in the space. If, as you work, you find yourself feeling irritated because some things are getting in your way, remove those items and put them aside to be addressed later. As mentioned in an earlier section, it is usually not a good idea to remove everything from a closet, if at all possible.

4. **Do an initial purge.** Look for "no brainer" items, things that you no longer love or use, and the bigger the better! Do a quick scan of the area you are clearing to see what jumps out at you as something you dislike, don't use, and are unlikely to use again. By getting rid of those items, you'll immediately shift energies in a positive direction and consequently feel encouraged by the progress you've made.

5. **Remove "no brainer" items to an area that you designate for items to donate or for trash.** If you are working on a closet in a room instead of a hall, don't leave the room! Put items to donate or throw away near the door or just outside the door.

6. **After that initial purge, start evaluating all other items in the closet, either by choosing to address whatever is easiest to clear or by tackling the biggest items in the closet.** For

example, the coats in a coat closet are usually the biggest items, but because you know you have specific sentimental feelings about some of the coats, you know it will be harder for you to start with the coats. Instead of starting with coats, you could start by sorting and evaluating the scarves, hats, and gloves. When you identify some hats, scarves, or gloves to donate and move them to the donation area, you'll be releasing their energy.

The energy shift that occurs whenever items are removed from a closet affects your energy. You are likely to feel encouraged by the progress you have made. The energy of the closet begins shifting from negative to positive. As the energy shifts, you'll likely feel less overwhelmed and more confident about making decisions about the coats.

7. **As you evaluate each item, ask yourself, "Do I love it? Do I use it?"** If the answer to both of those questions is "no," move the item to a donation pile.
8. **For those items that you do use or love, ask yourself, "Is this item still worthy of being in my space? Is it still in good condition?"** If your answers are enthusiastically, "Yes!!!," keep the item. If you feel any ambivalence about an item, that indicates that it is a low energy item and could be purged. Remember that keeping things with low energy could prevent you from getting more of what you really want in your life. Is that a risk you're willing to take?
9. **Make sure you save small items to evaluate last.** As I've said before, if you start trying to make decisions about small items at first, you'll be unable to see or feel any visible progress because the energy shifts will be tiny. Nothing will seem to

be changing for the better. You'll need reinforcement for the energy you are expending, especially in the beginning. So, resist the urge to deal with paper clips, matchbooks, and hair pins. Go to larger items like clothing, bottles of shampoo, blankets, and pillows.

10. **If you find yourself shutting down, paralyzed by overwhelm, stop and try to figure out the cause of your feelings.** Sometimes the cause is emotional. You may have encountered an item associated with a sad memory or with a person you loved who is no longer living. Sometimes you've inadvertently drifted to small items, so you aren't able to see much visible progress. Or, your brain could be exhausted from making so many decisions. Whatever the cause, take a short break. Take a deep breath, shake the tension from your shoulders, and begin again.

11. **As you empty things from the closet, start organizing what is left by clumping like items together.** Clumping helps create order and reduce overwhelm while you work. Don't be overly concerned with the final organization of the closet while you are clearing. Worry about how you'll get everything back into the closet could distract you from the clearing process.

12. **Once the clearing is done, remove the trash and any items to be donated to charities, family members, etc.** Removing those items from the space frees energy that is then available to you to use in the decision-making process for containerizing and organizing the things that will stay in the closet.

13. **Finish organizing the contents of the closet by clumping**

like items together and adding containers** to keep smaller items grouped together for visibility and easy access.
14. **Place everything back into the closet with items you use most often where they can be easily accessed.** Occasional use items can be stored on upper and lower shelves and on the floor.
15. **If after you put everything back in the closet you find that you have kept more items than will comfortably fit, go back and do a quick scan of the contents.** Go to categories of items that have duplicates. Tell yourself that you only want to keep the very best, that you don't need to keep everything that is useful. You can also ask yourself if you know anyone who might be able to use some of the items that you have in quantity. Relocate, give away or get rid of excess items.
16. **Once you have cleared the closet and reloaded it, step back and check to make sure that most items in the closet are visible.** If things aren't visible, you'll forget you have them. They will be "out of sight, out of mind." And, they won't be used. If they don't get used, why keep them?
17. **Once the closet is cleared and organized to your satisfaction, take a photo to document your hard work.** Pat yourself on the back for staying the course of clutter clearing to completion.

CHAPTER 14

Getting Help

"No one who achieves success does so without acknowledging the help of others. The wise and confident acknowledge this help with gratitude."
—Alfred North Whitehead

Now it's time to take action. Your brain (or the people around you) may be telling you that you should "just do it." After all, you now have this great resource with step-by-step information about what to do and how to do it. But, having information about what to do and doing it are two entirely different things.

When "just do it" doesn't work for you despite your best intentions and best efforts, and you are stuck, feeling overwhelmed by your clutter clearing and organizing challenges, it's time to call in the cavalry.

Getting help is something most people avoid. After all, fierce independence is part of our culture. Some people believe that if they know what to do and are physically capable of doing it, they should be able to do it.

I have watched countless people stay stuck or work far below their potential in their lives because they refused to get help. I too have struggled with the "I can do it myself" mentality (which reminds me of the words of a two-year-old in the middle of a tantrum). Then I realized that some very important things were not going to happen at all unless I got help.

Now when I find myself avoiding important tasks that affect my well-being or the well-being of my business, I hire someone to get me unstuck.

I am a firm believer that people should work within their areas of strength and hire people to do those things they:
- Hate doing
- Can't make themselves do
- Don't know how to do and don't care to learn how to do
- Are not capable of doing
- Are not good at doing

Being stuck in the process of clearing clutter and improving your space equates with being stuck in your life. Until you can see your way clear of the physical, mental, and emotional blocks in your environment, it will be difficult to move forward in your life.

Getting help could mean calling in a friend or family member to help you get started or hiring a professional to do the job with you. Following are the best support options to make clutter clearing happen.

Getting Help

Body Double

An economical way to get help is to find a body double. According to Judith Kolberg, author of *Conquering Chronic Disorganization* and co-author of *ADD-Friendly Ways to Organize Your Life*, a body double is a person who functions as a human anchor, someone who helps you focus and ignore distractions.

Having functioned as a body double hundreds of times with clients, it seems almost magical that clients who cannot face a task alone will tackle it with me present. My being there makes a difference.

Years ago, when my husband was working in a paper intensive job, he would occasionally reach crisis points and would ask me to come into his office to help him. At first, I thought he wanted me to organize his office for him. When I arrived, however, he invited me to take a seat in a chair in the corner of the room. He then went to work. He didn't need me to do the work for him or even with him; he just needed me to "be there" with him. Somehow my being there calmed his anxieties, so he could go to work.

A good candidate for a body double is someone who is willing to be with you while you work. It must be someone who understands that you are in charge of the process, and they are just there to hold the space to make it easier for you to work. They must be non-judgmental and supportive, as well as willing to do small but helpful tasks that you ask them to do. They must also be committed to helping you get things done, not socializing with you to the point of distraction. Parents, spouses, and siblings often do not make the best body doubles, because there are power struggles inherent in those relationships. Plus, some family members believe they are entitled to speak freely without considering the effect of criticism and judgment.

Supportive friends can make the best body doubles, especially those who also struggle with clutter and organization. Many clients have remarked that they can help friends and family members clear clutter and get organized, but can't seem to do it for themselves. That happens because it's not your stuff. It's easy to assist someone else because you don't have to deal with the normal thoughts and feelings that arise from the process.

Working with a friend also makes a clearing session a social event, and therefore more fun. When it's fun, you're more likely to get it done. Invite an understanding, empathetic friend to trade time with you. One day you both work in your home. Another day, you help her in her home. You'll both benefit and enjoy the process.

Professional Organizer

Most people balk at paying for the services of a professional organizer. They know they can do what's required to clear clutter. They are just not doing it. As I said earlier, knowing you can do something and actually doing it are two very different processes.

A professional organizer is someone with specific experience and training in the organizing process. Organizers most often work side by side with clients to clear clutter, organize what's left, and set up systems for maintaining order. Working with a competent organizer, you can accomplish as much as four times the clearing and organizing as you would on your own. Following is an example of my work with a client and the benefits she received.

My client asked me to help her clear her computer room that served a dual purpose as a repository of her daughter's school papers and school supplies. She had been so overwhelmed by the state of the space that she'd put off doing the job for months and months.

Following are the ways that I helped:
- **My presence helped her focus on the project.** After all, she was paying for my time, so she made time to get the work done. Also, just having someone by her side when she faced the clutter helped lower her anxiety. Anxiety stemming from the size of the challenge and not knowing how to address it had probably been blocking her from getting started.
- **I figured out where to start so we could see and feel immediate results.** I asked her to clear books from the overflowing bookshelf while I began restoring order in the rest of the room.
- **I kept the clutter clearing project moving** by periodically taking stock of our progress and making decisions about the order in which to tackle different areas of the room.
- **I kept track of time and prioritized the work** to get the most done in the allotted two hours.
- **I helped her make decisions about what to keep and what to get rid of** when she was uncertain.
- **I urged her to let go of many of the books.** When she hesitated to get rid of books because they belonged to her daughter, I reminded her that her daughter had outgrown many of the books and that she was not a saver (I knew that fact because I'd cleared clutter with her daughter in the past).
- **I sorted multiple bins of school supplies while she worked on the bookshelf**, something that would have been hard for

her to do because she doesn't naturally think in categories. She likely would have gotten overwhelmed by the quantity and variety of the supplies.
- **I directed her to where to work once she finished one project** and was uncertain where to go next for the most benefit.
- **I helped her clear the little stuff on one of the desks,** something that overwhelmed to her.
- **I came up with a storage plan for all the school supplies.** I then moved the supplies to their new homes, making sure they were all easily visible and in locations that provided easy access of the supplies that would be used most often.
- **I helped her finish up the project** by moving boxes of items to donate and bags of trash out of the room and straightening up the space.

We worked at a rapid clip for two hours. At the end of our time together, the room was in order and bags/boxes of items were outside the door, ready to be taken to the trash, to her workplace, or to a charity.

Could my client have made this kind of progress working on her own? Could she have done it in two hours? No way! She didn't even know where to start clearing, much less how to think about what should be kept and what she could let go of. The quantity of items and the chaos of the space was overwhelming and shut off her brain. Avoiding the space was so much easier than feeling overwhelmed and perhaps incompetent.

Working together as a team, with me directing the work, made all the difference. When we were done, she sighed with relief and had a big smile on her face. Working with a professional organizer came at a price, but it also helped her get the clearing done!

Getting Help

If you cannot get your clutter clearing done on your own, get help. The improvement in your space will affect your peace of mind and the quality of your life. To find a professional organizer in your area, go to NAPO.net, the website of the National Association of Professional Organizers. It has a great search tool for organizers based on location. Clear your clutter and make your home a comfortable place to come home to!

Coach

Hands-on organizing is very beneficial in the short run. However, if you want to learn to prevent the reoccurrence of clutter, how to clear clutter, and how to maintain an organized space on your own with non-judgmental support, coaching is your best option.

If you have been unsuccessful clearing clutter on your own or have worked with a professional organizer only to find that the disorganization returned again and again, and you want to make real progress to address your clutter challenges, go a step beyond hiring a professional organizer. Hire an organizer coach. A professional organizer can help you get the clutter clearing done, but your work with them does not necessarily result in the learning necessary to be able to clear clutter and maintain order on your own.

Organizer coaches are relatively new to the clutter clearing scene. They are professional organizers who have also been trained as coaches in Coach Approach (www.coachapproachfororganizers.com), a program developed by Denslow Brown in 2006. It received Accredited Coach Training Program status from the International Coaching Federation in 2015. Organizer coaches know how to clear clutter and organize spaces. Perhaps most important, however, they also know how to help people develop new, more effective habits and make empowering changes necessary for *sustaining* an organized, clutter-free environment.

Coaching is the single most powerful process for change I've ever experienced personally and with clients. I've performed hands-on organizing and clutter clearing since 1997. In that role, I usually direct the action and make sure progress is being made. Clients request hands-on organizing because they want **me** to improve their spaces. There is the possibility for change because as we clear clutter and organize a space, the energy in the space shifts from negative to less negative or positive, making positive change possible. However, that is a rather passive change process. Although clients receive the energy benefits of clearing clutter and getting organized, those benefits happen without much change or ownership by clients. Without ownership of the change process, clients are less likely and less able to commit to maintaining a clutter-free and organized space.

Coaching is a learning/action process that helps clients reach their goals. Unlike typical hands-on organizing, **the client** who is coached is the driver of the process of change. Clients reach out to me because they want something to be different and better in their lives. They want to be different—more productive, less scattered, more able to keep their homes and offices organized and clutter-free. They want to change what they are doing to get the results they seek.

I partner with coaching clients to co-create a relationship that makes it possible for them to find their own answers. For coaching to work, the client must want change and be willing to invest their time, energy and money in the process of coaching.

In coaching, clients have the opportunity to become more aware of who they are, what they do that either serves or doesn't serve them, what is important to them, what they're thinking, and their values and

Getting Help

strengths. That information and learning is then leveraged to develop effective strategies for action. With the client's permission I may offer possible strategies, but **the client** decides what action she will take between sessions. And, makes a commitment to act.

Accountability for action distinguishes coaching from professional organizing. It is an essential part of the process of coaching. Client agree to take specific action between sessions and report their progress in the next session. It is their opportunity to take their learning from coaching into real life practice.

For example, if a client wants to clear clutter from their bedroom, clearing bedroom clutter is identified as a goal. We then talk about the condition of the bedroom, particular challenge areas, previous attempts to clear clutter and their results, what is organized and what isn't. We then break down the big goal to clear bedroom clutter into individual steps to take to achieve it. Next the client chooses one of those steps to take between coaching sessions. We talk about the benefits of doing the task, possible obstacles to completing the task, and options for addressing obstacles. The client leaves the session with a specific step to take toward accomplishing their larger goal of clearing clutter from their bedroom, knowing that in the next session we will discuss what happened.

A coaching client has the opportunity to take steps to achieve her larger goal knowing that if she is unable to complete a task along the way, she will be able to return to coaching to process the experience, learn from it and identify other options for completing the task. My responsibility as coach is to provide accountability and support for the client by inquiring about what happened in the next session. Whether the client completed the action(s) or not, she has the opportunity to learn from whatever was or wasn't done. With learning and practice change occurs.

From Cluttered to Clear in Just One Year

CHAPTER 15

Last Words

*"Where we love is home, home that our feet may leave,
but not our hearts."*
—Oliver Wendell Holmes, Sr.

When you clear your home of clutter and create good feng shui, your life and the lives of anyone living in the home will change for the better. Those results may not be immediately obvious because sometimes you get results that are not what you expected.

For example, a woman came back from a feng shui class motivated to make changes that could shift energies in her home in such a way that she'd be able to communicate with her husband more effectively. She cleared clutter and organized her whole home, improving its feng shui. Almost immediately she and her husband had a long talk. Both decided that what was best was to end their marriage. She had hoped to repair their struggling marriage, but ultimately the best option was to let it go. As sad as it was to leave the marriage, this woman went on to find a very

From Cluttered to Clear in Just One Year

special man to marry and share her life with. Plus, unburdened by the sadness and angst of a failing marriage, she was able to find her true calling in a new business.

A final caution—for best results, clear clutter at a steady pace rather than at break-neck speed. Clearing always causes the energy of the space to shift. If done too quickly, without time and space for the energy to settle, your home and consequently your life can feel chaotic. One client experienced numerous things breaking in her home. Making changes too quickly can also cause physical illness. I got a cold after some rapid, overly-enthusiastic clutter clearing.

Pace yourself. Keep coming back. Get help if you need it. And, work until you once again love the look and feel of your home.

To contact Debbie Bowie:
www.DebbieBowie.com

www.ingramcontent.com/pod-product-compliance
Lightning Source LLC
Chambersburg PA
CBHW071651090426
42738CB00009B/1490